D1566664

From side hustle to main hustle to **Millionaire**

From side hustle to main hustle to **Millionaire**

13 lessons to turn your passion into a **passive paycheck**

Ryan Scribner

Publisher Mike Sanders
Editor Ann Barton
Art Director William Thomas
Senior Designer William Thomas
Proofreaders Georgette Beatty, Lisa Himes
Indexer Johnna VanHoose Dinse

First American Edition, 2022
Published in the United States by DK Publishing
6081 E. 82nd St., Suite 400, Indianapolis, IN 46250

See disclaimer, page 271

Library of Congress Catalog Number: 2022934276
ISBN 978-0-7440-6516-9

DK books are available at special discounts when purchased in bulk for
sales promotions, premiums, fund-raising, or educational use. For details,
contact: SpecialSales@dk.com

Printed and bound in the United states of America

For the curious
www.dk.com

MIX
Paper | Supporting
responsible forestry
FSC™ C018179

This book was made with Forest
Stewardship Council ™ certified
paper - one small step in DK's
commitment to a sustainable future.
For more information go to
www.dk.com/our-green-pledge

To my mom, for believing in me

Contents

Introduction

What is a side hustle? It's simply something that allows you to earn some extra money on the side. Think about it as a hobby that puts money in your pocket instead of taking it out. However, it's possible to take a side hustle a step further and turn it into a full-time business. Anyone with the desire to do so can start a side hustle today. What started out as a side hustle for me ended up becoming my full-time gig back in 2017. I quit my 9-to-5 job on a Monday afternoon and never looked back. However, as you will soon learn, it was a well-planned and calculated risk that I was taking. From there, I have slowly built a multimillion-dollar online financial content empire. The income from this has allowed me to make savvy investments in my personal life and given me the ability to prepare for future uncertainty. While I have spent most of the last five years providing viewers and readers with content about personal finance and stocks, I'll now be pulling back the curtains to give you an inside look at how this all took place, and how you too can follow in my footsteps.

Why Read This Book?

This book covers all phases of the side hustle journey, including the foundational groundwork that is required to give you the best chance of success. This isn't one of those books that blows smoke and tells you that everything I have done has been easy and that you can do it too. While it is entirely possible to emulate my strategies, you still have to put in the work—day in and day out.

For starters, we are going to be getting to the source of lazy habits. I was someone who struggled to stay motivated and stick with projects. If that sounds familiar, you have the correct book in your hand. It is crucial to tackle these lazy habits early on because they often become the reason behind our failures. I'll show you how to nip bad habits like procrastination in the bud for good. After that, we'll dive into the idea of "fake it till you make it" and how to control others' perception of you. This comes with an important caveat that you only use these techniques for purposes of good, as we will discuss when covering the Golden Rule.

Beyond that, we will be talking about the sacrifices required both early on and during your journey to get your side hustle off the ground. I'm not going to sugarcoat anything or tell you that it was easy for me to do this when I was in your shoes. I'll be sharing my real, firsthand experiences as well as the lessons that followed. One of the biggest sacrifices you will have to make when pursuing a side hustle is how you spend your time and your money.

As we will discuss later, these are the two most valuable resources you have available to you. The more time and money you waste, the less "fuel" you have for launching your business. As I learned from *The Richest Man in Babylon* by George Clason, it's important to remember that there is a big difference between what people make and what they keep. It doesn't matter how much you earn; you can still put yourself in a terrible situation financially. I turned this into a challenge to figure out how to keep as much of my money as possible. I'll be showing you how to get a grasp of your overall financial situation. Then, we will cover strategies for maximizing your rate of savings from this job to put toward your "freedom fund," assuming you want to follow in my footsteps one day and quit your job.

My side hustle of financial content on YouTube as well as blogging has taken me from working in a cubicle in upstate New York to becoming a millionaire in my mid-twenties. However, not everyone wants to follow in my exact footsteps as a content creator. Even if you do not want to create content, I will still be sharing my recommendations for the best side hustles to start right now. This includes both digitally based side hustles and "real world" side hustles, such as becoming a local tour guide. As you will soon learn, not all side hustles are created equally. There are specific characteristics I look for in a side hustle, and I will share those with you.

I will also introduce you to my specific technical strategies for getting off the ground with your new venture. The first is a set of recommendations for going out and making your first $100. Most people have a goal in mind of making thousands (if not tens of thousands) of dollars per month from their own side hustle or business. While this is a great goal, your very first goal should be to simply make $100. As the old saying goes, you need to walk before you run and crawl before you walk. I'll be showing you exactly how to crawl, or earn your first $100, before learning how to walk and then run. Beyond that, I will cover how to get your first 100 fans on social media. Even if you do not plan on creating content like I have, you still need to get people to care about your business. These days, having no presence on social media is the equivalent of not having a website. I'll show you my exact strategies for getting the ball rolling with both a website and social media. There are also a lot of platforms out there to potentially post content on. While I have had success with some, others have proven to be a waste of time for me. I'll be sharing with you which platforms are the most important today.

Everyone's characteristics for what they are looking for in a side hustle tend to be a bit different. What I was looking for with my side hustle, above all else, was freedom. In order to have that, I needed to be able to replace my income from my job, not just supplement it. I'll show you how I accomplished this step by step in a chapter on scaling your side hustle. Next, I will cover the important topics of hedging, diversification, and even selling your business. I know this may sound like a distant goal, especially if you haven't even started a side hustle. However, there are important considerations to be made on day one that can significantly impact the salability of your business. For example, if you create a content-based side hustle, are you going to be the face of it? This also has an impact on how passive or active the business is, both now and in the future. If you want to earn passively, you need to leverage the talents of others for content creation. I'll be showing you exactly how to do this.

I promise you nothing written within these chapters of my book is here to fill space. I would encourage you to read through all the chapters, even if you are already further ahead on your side hustle journey. Ultimately, this book will show you how I was able to become a millionaire in my mid-twenties starting with a simple side hustle. Here's a hint: it had almost nothing to do with luck. There's also something to be said about not being a flash-in-the-pan success. While some would argue that five years is not a long time to be self-employed, in the online community that is ages. Things move quickly online, meaning that you need to adapt in order to survive. By following the specific strategies outlined within this book, I have been able to consistently sustain a great living while growing my net worth for half a decade. In this same amount of time, I have seen many others rise to success but ultimately crash and burn.

Why Should You Care?

So, why should you care about a guy like me and my story? I am truly just a regular person from rural New York. No, not New York City—the "redneck" New York with all the farmland and tractors. If I, an average person coming from a middle-class upbringing, can accomplish this, there's nothing stopping you either. I used to think that success was something reserved for the select few, myself not included. As a result, I never pushed myself to do much in school. Years later, I learned that a lot of this was due to the limiting beliefs that I had internalized growing up. It's likely that you, too, may have these kinds of limiting beliefs. I was able to overcome my beliefs with the help of a mentor, which ultimately gave me the confidence to leave my "cushy" job at the time to pursue my dream. Later on, I'll share the many lessons my mentor taught me about getting past these negative beliefs. I will also be sharing how to find mentors in the real world who can help you on your side hustle journey.

I've read dozens of books on finance, money, and self-help, and I've found that there is a lot of regurgitated content out there. Essentially, authors are putting a new spin on an old idea. I promised myself that when I wrote my book, I would be sharing something unique. I feel like I have kept that promise, but I welcome you to be the judge of that. This is the story of my side hustle journey, exactly how it played out. I'll take you firsthand through the ups and the downs, teaching you the lessons that came along with the experiences.

Past-Due Bill Collections 101

First, I have to take you back to the year 2015. I was 20 years old with zero dollars in debt. I drove a vehicle that was older, but completely paid off. I also lived at home to keep my expenses to a minimum. A few weeks before graduating from community college with an associate degree in electrical construction and maintenance, I was offered a job as a past-due bill collector for my local power utility company at a rate of $27.20 per hour. Compared to my peers, this was an incredible rate of pay. I wasn't sure what I was getting myself into at the time, but I was up for the challenge. I spent the next six months driving all over upstate New York, shutting off power for customers with overdue bills.

Many people told me that I had it made with this job, but it didn't take long for me to realize that this was not the case. I was working at a union utility company with terrific benefits, or "bennies" as many at the company called them. Employees had exceptional pay, union protection, retirement, and job stability. In the rural bubble of upstate New York, my job was considered an excellent one. But once you venture out of the bubble in which you're raised and reframe your mind, you often find that things are not what they seemed to be. When I was younger, I had many interests and aspirations. I wanted to be a teacher or a college professor. Somewhere along the way, I completely lost sight of this and ended up getting paid $27.20 an hour to put myself in truly dangerous situations. I found myself doing something I hated. The job was taking an emotional toll on me, and I was undergoing a tremendous amount of stress for a paycheck. It was difficult to be the bearer of bad news and to see people struggling day in and day out. I had to really turn off my emotions. Years later, I found out that the woman who trained me and taught me the policy of "collect or cut" had ended up on medical leave after being hit in the face by an irate customer. I had a few close calls myself, but thankfully I was never injured.

This temporary position ended when cold weather hit because utility companies are legally obligated to keep services connected during extreme temperatures. I ended up bidding for a permanent job in the design department, and I was hired as a permanent employee in December 2015.

From 100 to 0 Real Quick

This was one of the strangest transitions of my entire life. Past-due bill collections was a very fast-paced job. I would visit 20 to 25 accounts a day, moving from house to house. It was the kind of job where you look at the clock and realize the day is half over and you haven't even had lunch. Design, on the other hand, was the complete opposite. This was by far the slowest and most mind-numbing job I had ever had. The pace of this work ended up being both a blessing and a curse. At first, it was not a good thing for me. I had entirely too much time on my hands and nothing to do. I came up with all sorts of tasks to pass the time, including alphabetizing my paperwork before shredding it. Some days, I would literally read the employee handbook cover to cover. Eventually, this lack of meaningful work sent me into a depression. I felt like I wasn't doing anything worthwhile in life. Sure, I was making good money, but I was missing fulfillment.

After a few months, I decided I was going to make the most of the free time I had. I began turning my cubicle into a mini classroom. I was adopting a frugal lifestyle and spending my downtime listening to podcasts and reading articles online about passive income and business ideas. I didn't know exactly what I wanted to do yet, but I knew that what I was currently doing with my life was not sustainable. Many of my friends and family members encouraged me to just stick it out, but I could not imagine spending five years of my life at this job, let alone 30. They were encouraging me to "do my time," as if I was in jail. Sure, I could have stuck it out, stayed for my 30-year sentence, and retired at 50. However, I was terrified of what I might lose in the process if I did that. I had already lost touch with my childhood dream of being a teacher, and I was afraid of how much more of myself I would lose over the course of my career. Would any part of myself be left at the end?

One of my favorite movies of all time is *The Shawshank Redemption*. It's about a man named Andy Dufresne who is sentenced to two consecutive life sentences for the murder of his wife and her new lover. But Andy didn't do it. One day, after being locked up for 27 years, Andy escapes. He leaves the prison through a tunnel he built behind a poster, chipping away at the concrete walls with a tiny rock hammer. So, just like Andy, I began planning my escape from my cubicle in Gloversville, New York. I viewed each podcast I listened to or article I read at my desk as slowly chipping away at the concrete walls of my prison with a rock hammer. Like Andy, I knew I had to keep things under wraps; otherwise the people in charge might have noticed me trying to escape.

My Passive Income Obsession

So, how did I escape? Like Andy, I was patient, slowly working toward that ultimate goal of freedom. However, I didn't have 27 years to spare. It all started with small changes in my daily routine and habits. I began reading a lot of books. This was something I hadn't done since high school. During my morning break, I had about 12 minutes of time to read. In those 12 minutes, I could read five pages of *Rich Dad, Poor Dad* by Robert Kiyosaki, a book recommended to me by my mentor, Jake Woodard. That book taught me many powerful concepts that I hadn't learned growing up. Although my dad taught me a lot about money, he was never a business owner. In fact, nobody in my family was. I was learning new principles and ideas that I hadn't been exposed to before. My biggest takeaway from this book was the idea of earning income 24/7 from multiple sources, instead of only earning money for eight hours a day, five days a week. As Kiyosaki teaches, the minute the workday ends, the 9-to-5-er stops earning income. On the other hand, those who have income from investments, real estate, and businesses continue earning money even while sleeping. I knew that if I ever wanted to amass true wealth, I would need to begin finding income streams outside of my job. I became obsessed with the idea of earning passive income.

It's hard to believe that your monthly earnings could equal what only the most highly educated individuals make in a year. I'm here to tell you it's true, it's possible, and I have done it myself. I started exploring different avenues for making money for one simple reason: freedom. I wanted freedom over my time and my location. I never bought into the idea of surrendering your life to an employer who tells you where to be and for how long. The only times I felt that I was actually living were when I would take vacations with friends and family. I remember walking on Old Orchard Beach in Maine on vacation, feeling happier than I had in months. Why be unhappy for 50 weeks out of the year in exchange for only two good ones? Later on, I decided to use all of my resources available to me to escape. I used my vacation days and sick time to spend even more time focusing on my side hustle.

I spent many months chipping away at the walls of society's prison with my proverbial rock hammer through self-education. Initially, I was spending most of my time learning about nutrition and personal development. I wanted to better myself overall. I had a long commute, so I was always listening to podcasts in my car and trying to learn as much as possible. One day, I picked up a few books related to swing trading. From that point forward, I became equally obsessed with the idea of stock trading. I would get up at 5:30 a.m., pack my lunch, and then listen to investing-related podcasts on the commute to work. After I finished my tasks for the day at work, which was usually around noon, I would take a walk during lunch and come back for my afternoon learning session. Then, on my commute home, more podcasts. After I got home, I would pack my stuff and go to the gym for a workout. Around 7 p.m., I would go home for a meal before going back out to a coffee shop. I would go to coffee shops every single night and read books about stock trading while taking detailed notes for two hours or so. On the weekends, I dedicated myself even more fully to my studies. I would catch up a little on sleep, get a workout in, and go right back to the books.

After a few months of doing this, I became very knowledgeable about the stock market, investing, and trading. However, the stock trading skills I was learning did not translate to real-world success in the financial markets. I decided to give myself a $500 budget for my trading account, which at the time was with Scottrade. This was long before commission-free trades were a thing, so I was paying $7.95 per trade. As you can imagine, this didn't leave much wiggle room for profit. I purchased a bank ledger notebook to log my trades in, and I placed trades from my phone at work.

Your Mistakes Can Make You Millions

I learned quickly that swing trading—trying to profit on two- to five-day trades with a $500 account while paying commissions—was not a great option for making money. Over the course of a month, I logged about 30 different swing trades in my bank ledger notebook.

Surprisingly, I didn't lose money. However, I started with a balance of $500, and after dozens of trades, I grew that account to a value of around $520. I looked down at all of my detailed notes in my ledger and thought about how much time I spent to make a profit of $20. At that point, I thought that swing trading would not be my ticket out. This, however, was not the case.

Swing trading wasn't the only money-making experiment I had tried. Another idea I had was buying used video games on Craigslist and flipping them on eBay. I ended up picking up an Atari console after work one day in an ALDI parking lot for $40. I also purchased over 100 assorted Xbox 360 games for $125 cash at a Walmart. I was initially going to sell the games individually, but soon realized how much work and trips to the post office that would involve. I ended up selling the Atari and turned a profit of roughly $11 after paying shipping and fees on eBay. Unfortunately, the other lot of video games turned out to be a money loser. I thought I was going to do well when the listing ended for a total of $160. However, shipping that many games cost me around $70. After paying shipping and seller fees, I was in the hole about $45. Overall, from the sale of these items, I had spent roughly four hours of my life to lose $34.

A lot of people have this misconception that those who are successful just wake up one day with a good idea and hit the ground running. Early missteps are actually very common. In fact, it's hard to even call them a misstep because I learned valuable lessons from everything I've ever tried. For the small handful of ideas that have made me a lot of money, I have had dozens of ideas that earned me nothing but experience. If you have tried and failed in the past, I am right there with you.

People tend to focus more on their wins than their losses. If you are having a conversation with a friend at the bar, they will most likely want to tell you about what is good in their life, not the negatives. Tying things back to the stock market, you hear a lot more about the winners in your friend's portfolio, not the other handful of stocks they lost money on. However, instead of looking at past experiences that didn't work as "losses," I prefer to simply file them under "experience." For example, years back when I was sucked into a multi-level marketing (MLM) business, I learned valuable networking skills and how to better vet an opportunity before committing myself to it.

I used to look at each one of these past side hustle endeavors as a failure. As a result, I would have less and less motivation each time I tried something new. This ultimately led to a feeling of helplessness, in which I was simply going to stick it out at a job I hated just for income. Do not make the mistake of looking at your past experiences and allowing them to dictate your future ones in a negative way. Every single person who is successful has had at least one really bad idea. You should not allow obstacles or failures you encounter to discourage you from continuing. I used to think that the path to becoming successful and eventually becoming a millionaire was relatively straight. The truth is actually the opposite.

The path is more like a game of Frogger; you've got to jump from one lane to the next, building upon previous ideas. Not every leap will be the right move in hindsight, but the important thing is to keep moving and keep adapting. Don't expect things to move in a straight line, especially early on.

A Big Idea

While I didn't profit directly from swing trading, I did become very knowledgeable on the subject. One day, I decided to type in "stock market" on YouTube. I ended up finding a video that someone younger than myself had uploaded called "Stock Market for Beginners." By the time the video ended, I realized I knew just as much as this guy, and possibly more in certain subject areas. I nearly jumped out of my seat when I saw how many views the video had, nearly 1 million. I had one of those "light bulb" moments for the first time in years. I could not believe a video that a college kid shot unscripted with low production got that many views. (Fun fact: that same video now has over 3.8 million views.) After clicking on a few other videos, I realized there was a massive opportunity here that only a few individuals had caught onto. In 2016, most people were still using YouTube as a place for entertainment. However, it was also becoming an educational platform. There was high demand for educational financial content and very little supply.

That evening after work, I made a stop on my way home. This time, it wasn't Barnes & Noble for more books, it was Best Buy. I ended up buying a cheap $250 digital camera to begin recording videos. I took the notes I had from all the books I read on swing trading and began turning them into short video lessons. At the time, I didn't have a professional studio or anything. I was completely bootstrapping it, so I decided to simply record these videos in my car. Not while driving, of course. During my lunch breaks at work, I would drive across the street and park behind Walmart. Then I would put my camera on the dashboard with a small tripod and press record. I had notes written out on Post-its that I would stick to my steering wheel. I would also record videos in my car from the parking lot of the gym before going in for my workout. Day by day, rinse and repeat, I recorded dozens of videos related to investing, personal development, and nutrition. However, I didn't post any of them right away. I wanted to come out of the gate with at least 50 videos when I started my channel.

From behind a Walmart in Gloversville, New York, my channel was born. And no, it was not an overnight success by any stretch of the imagination.

You Can't Be Lazy in Business

Let's go back to the summer of 2006, when I started a lawn mowing business with the support of my parents, grew it to three clients, and then ran it into the ground. The experience taught me one of the most important lessons of business: don't be lazy.

I was 11 years old, it was officially summer, and I had decided to satisfy my boredom by making money. I first attempted to sell my unwanted Game Boy Advance games to the neighborhood kids. I threw in the towel with that idea after my door-to-door sales tactics drew strange looks from the other kids. Instead, I asked my dad if he would teach me how to use the lawn mower. He showed me how to use the self-propelled push mower, making sure to leave a little overlap with each pass to avoid missing any grass. Once I learned how to mow the grass, I asked him if I could start a neighborhood business clipping lawns. He agreed to pay me $20 to clip our lawn and even offered to pay for all the gas required as his contribution toward the business.

I wheeled out on my Razor Scooter and placed flyers in the mailboxes. The next day, I ended up getting a few calls back! Two of my neighbors were interested, and they both agreed to pay me above the $14 price on my flyer, which was very nice. One neighbor offered to pay $20 and the other said they would pay $25. In addition, one told me I could use their riding lawn mower as long as it was okay with my parents.

Excuses, Excuses, Excuses

I had a pretty sweet gig. I would mow the three lawns each week and pocket $25 with zero expenses. But I was very lazy. I would often push the mower down the street to my first customer, mow half the lawn, and get tired. I would then go home halfway through, complain to my mom, eat a few cheese sticks, and watch cartoons for a few hours with my brother. On multiple occasions, I didn't even return to finish the job until the next day. You would think I did a better job at the house with the riding mower, seeing as I just had to sit on it and steer. Nope. I would still come up with an excuse to put off mowing the grass every single week. One day, after pulling yet another lame excuse, I biked over to the client's house and my stomach dropped. My client was outside on the riding mower doing the lawn himself! I was officially canned. He told me that he simply could not rely on me being there to mow the grass. I really couldn't argue with him on that one.

By then, it was the middle of the summer and I had only two clients left. My dad was also very unhappy with my lazy mowing. I wasted so much time monkeying around with the neighbors that I barely got the lawn done at home. I was soon off lawn duty entirely at my house. By the end of the summer, I would also lose the client who was paying me $20 to mow with my push mower. However, the reason for being canned was different this time around.

It was a hot August day, and I could not fathom pushing the mower down the street and mowing in the sun. Instead, I came up with a better idea. I knew that my dad had a broken riding mower, but I was wondering just how broken it was. I went into our shed, filled it with gas, and turned it on. I drove the riding mower down to the neighbor's house, convinced that it was not in fact broken. What I hadn't realized was that one side of the deck had come loose from the frame, so the mowing deck was completely crooked. Despite that, 11-year-old me was convinced that he had come up with an easy solution to his mowing problem. I proceeded to mow the entire lawn with this riding mower. Honestly, I knew something was wrong after the first few passes. The left side was cut almost down to the dirt and the right side was cutting normally. That was the last day of my mowing business.

Lazy Habits for Life

Laziness seems to be something that we all struggle with, but it tends to show up in different ways. You can get away with being lazy at work for the most part. That is because when you work at a job, you are just one component of the overall operation. There are systems of checks and balances to ensure that things run efficiently. You might not know you have these lazy habits while working for someone else, because the systems in place allow for things to be smoothed over. For a lot of people, the process of starting a side hustle and doing something completely on their own reveals their lazy habits. That is because, instead of being one component of the overall operation, you become the entire operation. If John from customer service isn't returning emails in time, you can blame John. However, when you are the sole operator of a business, you can only blame yourself. At the end of the day, a side hustle is a mini business. Someday, it might even become your entire business. However, the success you have with the business largely comes down to your own lazy habits. Starting a side hustle puts the full responsibility of operations on your shoulders.

Unfortunately, my lazy habits did not end that summer. I would end up running into them headfirst years later after I went full-time with YouTube. When I switched to YouTube as a full-time job, I was making just enough money from ad revenue to get by. At the time, I was following the strategy of producing more and more content. Or, to be blunt, "throwing shit at the wall and seeing what sticks." Although I was only posting three videos weekly, I planned on roughly doubling my output to five to seven videos per week. My thought process was that producing more videos would, in turn, increase viewership and double my income. What I did not consider was the stress that this would put me under, or the lazy habits that would consequently reemerge. Most people have a similar experience to mine when starting their own business. Maybe you aren't lazy, but we all have our own good and bad habits. These habits tend to emerge when you are "running the show," or handling the business completely on your own.

My laziness doesn't always stem from a lack of desire to do something. Instead, it often emerges when I try to do too many things at once. Once I decided to double my output of videos, I immediately began cutting corners. I stopped putting as much thought into my outlines, rushed the research, and ditched my recording studio.

A Very Bad Idea

A decent amount of work goes into producing video content. The first step is to determine a topic. After that, you either write out a general outline or a detailed script. Then, you record the video, edit the video, create the thumbnail, fill out the metadata, and click publish. I had a good recording setup at the time in the spare bedroom at my mom's house. I had purchased a whiteboard from Staples, put it up on a wall with some different posters, and set up a few soft box lights for good lighting. But, as we didn't have central air, I would have to run a window air conditioning unit for an hour or two in the room before recording videos. This required a little bit of planning around the time of video recording because I had to account for this cool-off time. I soon made the decision to ditch the recording studio altogether and record videos from my bedroom. Instead of having good lighting and a somewhat legitimate looking set behind me, I now had a closet door and a messy shelf as my backdrop. However, this meant that I could outline a video and immediately record it without worrying about cooling off my recording space. In my mind, I was doing things as efficiently as possible to increase my output. I ended up recording videos like this for about a week.

Immediately after posting the first video, I received terrible feedback from my audience. They were all asking why I had ditched my studio in exchange for a messy bedroom. I really had no good answer that I could share with them. Unfortunately, the trouble didn't end there. Since I was focusing so much on quantity, the outlining process suffered. The time I used to spend researching and creating an outline was cut in half. Not only did the content suffer tremendously, I ended up getting a copy-right strike on my channel.

I had found an interesting article that I thought would be a good topic for a video. However, instead of pulling information from multiple sources, I based my lazy research on one article. While I did include my own thoughts, the other information I presented was quite similar to the referenced article. Although I had included a link to the article in my video description, that was not enough to keep me out of trouble. At the end of the week, I received an email about a copyright strike on my channel, stating that my video followed the article too closely. That was one of the most gut-wrenching and agonizing weekends of my entire life. I really don't think I slept. Here I was trying to make it on YouTube after quitting my "cushy" job, and just a few months in, my bad strategy put my entire channel in jeopardy. Laziness, or cutting corners, does not always stem from a desire to do little. In my case, it was a result of trying to do too much. However, there is no excuse for plagiarism, or copying someone else's work.

You Quit Your Job for This?

Despite posting a new video every day that week, none of my new content was doing well. After getting the copyright strike, I went through the comments on the videos I had posted that week. Most of the feedback was negative, but one comment really hit home: *Dude … you quit your job for this.*

I was honestly embarrassed with the content I was putting out there. I quit my job to focus more on my channel, but this push for more content and maximum efficiency put my entire business in jeopardy very early on. I had other embarrassments beyond that week spent shooting videos in my bedroom. I once made a video about "drone business ideas" without remotely considering FAA regulations and got absolutely roasted in the comments. It was another perfect example of under-researched and lazy content, a video filled with nonsense ideas I had come up with for businesses that would not even be legal.

When it comes to business, there is no room for laziness. No matter what the reason is, even if you are just making bad short-term decisions like I was, you need to prevent your lazy habits from interfering with your business. Am I completely free from all my lazy habits today? Nope. I don't think that is even a realistic goal. It took me a while to fully embody this, but I now only allow myself to do something if I am able to give it my all. When it comes to a side hustle, you don't want to just be decent at what you do. You want to put your best foot forward. This is especially true if you plan on creating any type of online content. While it's certainly not impossible to start and grow an online platform right now, it is very competitive. If you are creating lazy content, there is someone else out there who isn't. In the long run, they will win.

Four Strategies to Combat Lazy Habits

Over the last few years, I have come up with a few strategies to help me combat lazy habits and procrastination. If you are anything like me, you may find that your lazy habits creep back in over time. These strategies help to combat, or fight back, against these habits. I don't think it's a realistic or attainable goal to fully rid yourself of these habits forever. As a result, you may need to revisit this section from time to time.

1. COMPLETE TASKS BACKWARD

Most of us have a general idea of the tasks we need to complete each day, yet many of us still push them off endlessly. Once you start your side hustle, you will have new tasks related to your business to work into your schedule, in addition to everything else you are already doing. Based on our preferences, our brains are programmed to do our most favorable activities first. That often leaves everything that we don't want to do for the end of the day. By that point in time, you are likely tired from the tasks completed earlier and have little drive to complete the tasks that you don't enjoy. You might even just decide to push those tasks off for another day.

Therefore, the best solution I have found is to complete your tasks in the exact opposite order that you want to do them in, from least favorable to most enjoyable. Procrastination tends to come into play when we keep pushing off the things that we don't want to do. When you complete tasks in the opposite order, you save what you are most excited about for the very end. Not only will this encourage you to get the less desirable tasks done, but it also ensures that you have more energy for the tasks that usually burn you out the most.

Here's how to put this strategy into action. Every day, I write a list of three to five things I want to complete. Then, I write a number next to each task based on the order that my brain wants to do them in. Usually, creative tasks such as recording videos end up high on the list, while more mundane tasks end up lower. After that, I work through the list backward and complete tasks in the opposite order, from the lowest rated to the highest. I have found this to be one of the most effective strategies for minimizing stress and making sure all the important tasks related to my business get done. Procrastination usually leads to a lot of anxiety related to not completing tasks. This can also have a spiral effect, where continuing to push tasks off further and further to a later date leads to more anxiety. By the time you get around to completing whatever task you've been pushing off, you probably spent twice as much time worrying about it. This has been the perfect solution for me to get things done without procrastination or anxiety. I hope it works for you too. However, for this strategy to work, you need to actually follow what you have outlined for yourself. Above all else, discipline is the most important trait required for success in anything that you do. That discipline is built over time with yourself by simply following your own word.

2. CONSIDER "WHY" YOU DO THINGS

The next strategy is to remind yourself of the "why" behind your side hustle. When I get too caught up in the numbers of my different businesses, I find that I need to take a step back and remember why I am creating content online. My father is a financial advisor, so I've been learning wise money habits since I was a child, and I always wanted to be a teacher. The "why" behind my channel is to create content that can help those who are not financially savvy, while enjoying a sense of fulfillment in the process from my work. Bad financial habits are almost always a result of not having access to good financial information. I want to help those who didn't have the same opportunities that I had while growing up to learn about money. When I think about my "why," I remember that this isn't just something that I do to make money.

This is another reason why it's so important to focus your side hustle on something that you are passionate about. When your side hustle relates to something you are naturally interested in, it is far easier to stay motivated and continue working on it. I have always been interested in personal finance and the stock market. In my down time, I still watch YouTube videos and read books to continue learning more and more. But in the past, I tried many different side hustles where my main motivation was to make money. I was pretty good at getting things off the ground, but I lacked the follow-through. A lot of this had to do with the fact that I was not actually interested in these past ventures. I once tried starting a blog about natural testosterone-boosting supplements. However, I got completely burned out. I had no interest in learning about supplements, so it was an exhaustive process of researching and writing about something I didn't care about. If you force yourself to do something you don't enjoy in order to make money, you will have a much more difficult time keeping yourself motivated. Even if you do have the discipline to keep going, this path is unlikely to bring you fulfillment, a very important aspect of life.

3. FIGURE OUT WHAT IS IMPORTANT TO YOU

There is a quote from Confucius that I love, "A man who chases two rabbits catches neither." If you focus your efforts on multiple ventures at once, your time, attention, and resources will be split among them all. Remember that most businesses do not succeed; you simply cannot afford to split your focus and resources. Just one of these ventures will require all of your effort in order to have a chance to thrive. When the time is right, you have to go all in on one thing—you can't try to build multiple side hustles at the same time. But wait, doesn't the average millionaire have multiple streams of income? Yes, they do. However, most of them, including myself, built each income stream one at a time. This advice to establish multiple streams of income has caused a lot of confusion and corresponding bad execution in the entrepreneurial community. I frequently come across individuals who think that they are doing the right thing by trying to build multiple revenue streams at the same time. This is the equivalent of chasing two or more rabbits at the same time. You will be going home empty-handed. Instead, your goal in business should be to build up one revenue stream, have it managed by someone if needed, and then move on to creating the next one. While I now have multiple successful blogs and social media platforms, these were largely built one at a time. In addition, circling back to social media, you need to conquer one singular platform first. If you try to be a YouTuber, blogger, podcaster, and a TikToker at the same time, you will 100 percent burn yourself out while simultaneously spreading yourself too thin. Instead, master one, then divert your audience and some of your attention to the next platform.

To figure out what is important to you, I recommend a simple process of elimination. In Lesson 5, I discuss a time-management strategy that essentially involves self-auditing your time. Once you know how you spend your time day to day, you can go down the list assigning a priority to each thought or action. After that, eliminate the low-priority thoughts or actions that aren't helping you reach your more immediate goals. This doesn't mean that you are giving up on thoughts and actions forever; it just means that you aren't focusing on them right now.

4. REWARD YOURSELF

My last strategy to combat laziness is the simplest one: give yourself a reward after you complete a certain task. What this reward will be is going to be different for everyone; I find that I am often motivated by a cold beer or a good meal. For example, you could decide that you are going to "crack a cold one" after you work through your to-do list. Having some type of reward can be a very motivating factor.

However, you must be disciplined enough to know when to reward yourself. If you get all your work done, go get your reward. If you push the last few things off and procrastinate, don't reward yourself. Starting a side hustle and getting it off the ground is going to require discipline. This is something that many of us are lacking. You will have days where you decide to skip the late-night work session in lieu of some form of entertainment. However, in order to build that discipline needed to succeed in business, you cannot allow yourself to receive the reward you had set for yourself after working. If you told yourself you would have a beer after getting your work done but you didn't do the work, don't crack one open. Sorry, no soup for you. This is the only way to build discipline with yourself. Your future self will thank you.

The Quality Bar

While I was able to get away with somewhat lazy content in 2017, that would not be possible today. This is largely due to the changes in the levels of supply and demand between when I was first creating content on YouTube and today. Am I saying this to discourage you from creating online content? Nope. I'm attempting to convey just how much of an overwhelming supply of content there is out there today. In the online world, there is something that we refer to as the quality bar. This is the minimum level of quality your content needs to meet in order to compete within a given niche. The more popular a niche is, the higher the quality bar. For example, one of my YouTube friends, Nate O'Brien, travels all over the world, so I asked him why he didn't consider making travel vlogs of his adventures. He told me that he had thought about it before and had determined that the quality bar was just too high. In order to compete with the existing travel content out there, he would need at least $20,000 worth of camera equipment along with the know-how. Professional travel influencers use video equipment like gimbals and drones that have a relatively large learning curve associated with them. It would be difficult, if not impossible, to compete with them without using the same equipment. Beyond that, the editing involved with most travel videos is very advanced.

When I was making my first videos on YouTube, my production quality was pretty low. (This was especially true when I was recording the videos from my bedroom during that bad week!) However, at that point in time, the quality bar for content in my niche was low too. A low supply of content related to financial topics meant the demand was just beginning to emerge. Keep in mind that this was before commission-free trading apps like Robinhood went mainstream, which led to a surge of retail trader interest. Since I was early on that wave, I had a first-mover advantage. I was able to get away with lower production quality due to the low quality bar. That would not be possible today in the personal finance niche.

The internet does not need any more lazy content. It is not about how much content you can produce; it is about creating the best possible piece of content on a given topic. The cream rises to the top. So, if you are considering creating online content, the very first step is to determine the quality bar of that niche. That usually means researching the area you're interested in. At that point, you must determine whether or not you can meet, or hopefully exceed, the existing quality bar.

What if you have no interest in making online content as a side hustle? Fortunately, the same quality bar analogy holds true when starting most businesses. For example, if you start a service-based side hustle, you should still determine the current quality bar for this service in the local area. That could mean calling for quotes, browsing websites, and checking social media as well as any digital ad campaigns. Long before you start working on the ins and outs of your side hustle, you should be conducting research on what it is that you want to be doing. In my case, this meant watching hours of videos from financial creators like Jack Chapple and Financial Education on YouTube. At the time, these were the only people doing videos in my niche. I had to understand what it is that they were offering to make sure I could compete with them and even put my own spin on things. If you have some ideas on what you want to do now for a side hustle, you can begin this research phase anytime. I recommend simply taking notes in a journal.

Key Takeaways

- Start your side hustle with the intention of being the very best at whatever you do. Why aim for mediocrity?
- When your side hustle relates to something you are naturally interested in, it's far easier to stay motivated.

Consider your passions when choosing your side hustle.

- Build your income streams one at a time.
- Complete tasks backward to "trick" your brain, eliminating the potential for procrastination.
- Consider rewarding yourself when you complete tasks throughout the day.
- Take time to figure out your "why" behind starting your side hustle. This will be your long-term source of motivation.

Dress Yourself (and Your Business) for Success

Learning how to use perception to your advantage is one of the most important skills to master in life. But it's not about misleading people. Instead, it's about representing yourself and your business in the most professional manner possible. Everyone out there is guilty of judging a book by its cover in some form, even if we don't share our judgments out loud. You want people to have the very best possible first impression of both you and your business. Fortunately, this is something you have a lot of control over.

How you dress and carry yourself has a huge impact on how others interact with you. Beyond that, how you dress your business will have an impact too. By that, I am referring to things such as a professional website, custom domain, and other aesthetic elements that impact the user experience. These things make a huge difference in terms of how others perceive your business. I learned this lesson about appearance and perception when I worked at my first job. A few years after my failed lawn mowing business, I decided to get a part-time job. My parents had recently gone through a divorce and our lifestyle had changed quite a bit. Since my parents were having their own financial struggles, I wanted to make sure I wasn't a burden on them whatsoever financially. So, 15-year-old me decided to get his working papers and apply at the local grocery store.

Failed Grass Clipper to Grocery Bagger

I spent a lot of my summer at the grocery store. I remember being impressed that I was making $7.30 an hour, $0.05 above minimum wage at the time. I enjoyed the early morning weekend shifts. Fathers, including mine on occasion, would come in before 8 a.m. for the newspaper, a bag of coffee grounds, and freshly made bagels that were still warm. It wasn't busy yet in the store, so you had a chance to have an actual conversation with people. I didn't really think much of how I was dressing back then, other than the fact that I wanted to be as professional as possible at my first job. We had company-issued red polo shirts with the store logo on them, but the pants were up to you. The only requirement was that they had to be tan. I decided that I wanted to dress top-notch, so I went out and purchased a few pairs of tan khaki pants. I also had a pair of dress shoes that I had purchased secondhand from the Salvation Army, so I decided to wear these along with a Citizen watch that my mom had bought me. (At the time, my mom and I were doing a lot of clothes shopping at the Salvation Army, as well as couponing to save money and make the most of what we had.) Just about every other guy my age at the grocery store wore sneakers, an untucked store polo shirt, and tan jeans of some kind. I really stood out with my pants, dress shoes, khakis, watch, and tucked-in polo shirt. I would also gel my hair before going to work to look more professional. It didn't take long for me to get the nickname "Mr. President."

Dressing for success began to have some very clear benefits for me. There was supposed to be a scheduled rotation at the grocery store for "cart duty," going out and gathering the loose carts in the parking lot. During the summer, when the temperature could get above 100 degrees Fahrenheit, cart duty was a very undesirable task. You did get access to a free cooler of bottled water, but that was just about the only perk. I began to notice that I was never included on the cart rotation. All of the workers would be assigned to either carts, register, or bagging at the start of their shift, and I was always told to go to a register. On one occasion, the front-end manager came over to me and told me that there was a no-show and that they needed someone to go out and do carts. I hadn't done cart duty in the two months I had been working there, so I figured I was due. However, something funny happened instead. While the front-end manager was explaining the process and showing me where the reflective vests were, the store manager came over to us. He pointed down at my dress shoes and said to the front-end manager, "You aren't really gonna make him push carts in dress shoes, are you? He's gonna ruin them." Remarkably, the front-end manager ended up going out and taking care of cart duty for the few hours that there was no coverage. It was at that point in time that I realized the way you dress and carry yourself can have a huge impact on how people perceive and interact with you. This, in turn, has an impact on your individual life experiences.

Perception Is Reality

After I left my grocery store job at the end of the summer, I took a temporary holiday position at JCPenney that would end up lasting over two years. During that time, I learned more about perception, particularly as it relates to personal appearance. At JCPenney, most customers visiting the men's suit department were getting clothes for a job interview. On a regular basis, I would help people of all ages figure out what clothing they needed for the big day. This usually required measuring neck and sleeve sizes, something most people don't usually know offhand. It was always remarkable to see the transformation in someone's confidence after they put on nice, well-fitting clothes. Nothing about the person changed other than their clothing. However, in a sense, everything about them changed when they put on their new outfit.

Focusing on your appearance makes you seem more professional and confident to others. In most cases, I have always found that when you look good, you feel good. In fact, I keep this trick in my back pocket for days that I don't feel motivated. When I'm feeling down on myself, I will usually force myself to put on some nice clothing and cologne. Almost immediately, I find myself feeling more confident and motivated. When I started my YouTube channel in 2016, I knew that I was going to need to dress myself for success. I would be creating videos that were going to be viewed by people of all ages, so I needed to make sure I looked the part. I applied a lot of the knowledge from my time at JCPenney, and I wore many of the clothes I purchased there years ago with my employee discount.

Let me give you an example of how to use perception to your advantage in order to get ahead. In one of my efforts to create multiple income streams, in 2019, I purchased a multifamily property in upstate New York. I was following the principles I had learned reading *Rich Dad, Poor Dad*, creating another income stream for myself. (Later on in Lesson 11, we will talk more about this strategy I followed called "house hacking.") The property I purchased had a guest cottage that needed to be remodeled. The structure had plumbing and electrical hooked up, but it was otherwise a total shell. This was going to be a big project and I needed to find the right person for the job. I liked the way that the mirrors, lights, and walls had been done at my barbershop, so I asked my barber for his contractor's name. When I met the contractor, Derik, a few days later, he showed up right on time. I was immediately impressed by his clothing, promptness, and truck. He had a newer Ford F-150 and wore a pair of dress shoes, fitted pants, and a button-down shirt. Conversationally, he was very confident and carried himself well.

We all make assumptions about someone based on their appearance. I'd be a liar if I told you I didn't make assumptions too. Judging Derik by his cover, the stylish clothing showed me he cared about himself and took care of his appearance. That, and the new truck with his business logo on the side, made me confident in his ability to get the job done. After meeting Derik, I was very impressed and decided to work with him for the project. Since he had dressed himself and his business, Choice1 Renovations, for success, I cut him a check for $10,000 as a deposit that day. Overall, the remodel project was completed within a reasonable amount of time, and I was very happy with the outcome.

It wasn't until Derik and I became closer friends a few years later that I learned that my guest cottage and the barbershop had been two of his biggest projects to date. I never would have guessed that based on the professional work, invoices, and other factors. I ended up telling him that I decided to work with him based on my first impression of him and his business. He laughed and told me that is exactly why he drives a newer truck and buys nice clothing. He understood fully how perception works and was able to use that to his advantage. Since then, our relationship has grown. Derik has helped me out a ton with different projects, including a house flip in Miami Beach. As a result of this good first impression and subsequent quality work, I've done hundreds of thousands of dollars' worth of business with him. In addition, I've sent him tens of thousands of dollars' worth of referrals.

Unfortunately, not everyone out there is using perception to their advantage. Focusing on the wrong kind of perception can have a negative outcome, especially financially. As a result, it is important to understand the difference. Let me give you an example of focusing on the wrong form of perception. When I was working for the power utility company, I noticed that most of the employees drove brand-new trucks. This was so common that there was a running joke about how long it would take a new hire to go out and buy a truck after being hired. Since I drove an almost 20-year-old SUV, I caught a lot of flak from others. There was constant peer pressure to go out and spend your money. Many of these employees with newer trucks could have driven older vehicles, but they preferred to drive new ones. For the most part, this decision was all about how their peers viewed them. I have found that this type of perception matters very little in life. This "keeping up with the Joneses" mentality ends up becoming a financial trap for almost all who participate. It's a game that nobody wins. Perception does matter—just not in the sense of impressing friends or others around you. Spending money in pursuit of impressing others or maintaining some type of image is a losing strategy. You are wasting your most important resource as a result.

Now that you understand the power of perception, begin considering how you can use this to your advantage. The idea isn't to be misleading, but instead to present yourself as the best version of yourself that you can possibly be. That could mean spending a few weeks or even months focusing on yourself and your skills before starting a side hustle, just like I did. You are better off spending many months preparing for battle, instead of jumping in headfirst without being prepared.

The Skill Improvement Game

Many of us know that we need to make improvements in our lives, but it is difficult to get the ball rolling. Instead, we often spend our time repeating bad cycles over and over. I was no stranger to this in my teenage years. When I was younger, the only thing I was really passionate about was video games. I would spend hours playing games like Skyrim. When you first start out in the game, you choose a character based on their skills. As you progress, you lean on your strengths while also focusing on the skill areas you need to improve upon. Eventually, you master the skills required to beat the game. My problem was that I was too focused on my video game characters and not focused on real life. I was out of shape, disengaged in school, and skating by for the most part. My mom always saw potential in me, but it had yet to surface for a sustained period of time. My love for school and teachers faded in middle school, and by high school, it had disappeared.

It wasn't until I made this connection that everything changed. We, as human beings, are a lot like these characters from Skyrim as well as other video games. When we reach adulthood, many of us have leveled up in certain skill areas but have neglected others. However, what most people do not realize is that, just like video game characters, we too can level up our skills. Instead of wasting hours on a character in a game, become the character in your own game of life. Would you really have your character just sitting there on the couch all night? If you focus on a skill that you need to improve on, in a short period of time, you will be able to "level up." Sure, you won't have fancy charts to follow your progress like you would in a video game, but it is nevertheless an extremely motivating and rewarding process to improve upon skills within your life.

Once I drew this parallel between video games and real-life skill development, I ditched the games altogether. I wanted to go all in on the game of life. This led to a lot of changes in my life over time. On top of focusing on my physical appearance with things like professional clothing and nice haircuts, I also began working on a few other skills, like my speaking ability. This is something that a lot of people do not consider, but the tonality and projection you use with your voice when recording a video or podcast is far different than having a conversation with a friend. I knew I was going to be a bit camera shy at first on

YouTube, so prior to even starting my channel, I started doing vocal exercises in my car. When most people hear this, they probably think of singing. However, there are a lot of exercises that help you with things such as tonality and enunciation. I would listen to YouTube videos and practice the exercises on my commute to and from my job at the power utility. For weeks, I would drive to and from work in my beat-up SUV practicing tongue twisters.

My favorite place to learn new skills and improve old ones is none other than YouTube. There are now thousands of people making videos about every topic imaginable. Whether it's learning how to close a sale or whiten your teeth, you can "level up" all of these skills using free information found on the internet. In a way, that is what my channel and blogs do for other people. During this self-improvement portion of my life, I felt that I was preparing myself for battle. I needed to make sure I was the best possible version of myself before starting something again. I had tried and failed many times in the past with business ideas and even other YouTube channels. I knew this time had to be different, so I prepared myself in every way possible.

Your Routine Is Everything

Contrary to popular belief, the act of starting a side hustle isn't going to magically change you into a different person. You'll be the same person you are today, but with a lot more going on. Spending a few months focusing on your skills could put you years ahead. However, this all depends on where you are currently in your life. If you are generally happy day to day and feel that your life runs smoothly, you could be ready to start a side hustle now. On the other hand, if you feel completely unhappy and think that your life is a mess, starting a side hustle is just going to add more stress on top of this. It's kind of like getting a new pet. If you have prepared yourself fully, it can be an overwhelming positive in your life. But if you have no routine and buy a pet impulsively, the pet's going to add more stress to your life after the "new factor" wears off.

I have found that a fitness routine is a great precursor to starting a side hustle, as it teaches you how to have self-discipline. The concept here is pretty simple: if you don't stick to your gym routine, you probably won't stick to your side hustle either. If you don't strengthen your skills in that given area, your bad habits will begin creeping in. For example, if your life is cluttered and disorganized, odds are your business will be too. Before starting a side hustle, I recommend that most people have some type of routine exercise that they complete daily. This could mean going to the gym or simply taking a walk. If you have pets, you should have a routine with them as well because they can become a major distraction. Doing these things allows you to lay a foundation for success. I lacked discipline before I made fitness a priority in my college years. It was the day-in-and-day-out repetitions that taught me how to "tough it out." Not to mention, I always have more motivation and energy on the days that I exercise.

How to Dress Your Business

Beyond your physical appearance and attributes, it is equally important to focus on the appearance of your business. Think back to the lesson on the quality bar. That bar has been pushed higher and higher with all the new tools and resources available today. It has never been cheaper and easier to represent yourself professionally online. However, you should not view that as a discouraging statement. Instead, you should be encouraged. It is just as easy for you to go out there and lean on the shoulders of experts just like others have before you. You don't need a background in coding to have a website. You simply need a great website person.

With $100, you can get started with a logo, a domain name, and an email ending in your personal domain instead of using a Gmail address. People tend to associate "@gmail.com" with a personal email address. If you use it for your side hustle, it gives the impression that you have a hobby, not a business. For most of this, I recommend leveraging the skills of freelancers via websites like Fiverr. This is a platform that allows you to hire someone for remote work, starting for as little as five dollars per project. Unless you have a real passion for graphic design, it's not worth it to make a logo yourself. There are thousands of people who do this kind of thing full-time, and odds are, they are much better at it than you. It won't cost you very much either, maybe $50. You can also feel good about supporting someone else's side hustle in the process.

When it comes to making your business look professional, a lot of it is common sense. For example, use the same fonts across your logo, website, and social media presence. In addition, use the same small handful of colors consistently. Another suggestion is to go out and get some professional headshots taken by a photographer. This will come in handy down the road in many applications. Eventually, you will want to create something called a "brand style guide" for your business and brand. This is a digital document outlining everything about the look and feel of the brand, including color schemes and other important details. For now, aim to work with a freelancer to come up with a basic color scheme, font, and logo. Having gone through multiple rebrands across my different businesses over time, I can tell you it is no easy process. You are far better off to take the time to sit down and figure out these details before ordering business cards, creating a website, or doing other things related to the visuals of your brand.

Even if you are not going to be creating content online, you still need a website. I can't think of any business today that wouldn't need one. That doesn't mean everyone has one, of course. However, that means you will have a clear advantage over some of your competitors by having a professional website. In addition, social media is very important for almost all businesses too. If you have to choose just one, I recommend focusing on Instagram. However, it's important to build followings on other platforms over time, because Instagram isn't likely to be the top dog forever. Ten years from now, it will likely be a totally different platform that commands the most eye-balls. If you start a service-based side hustle, Instagram is going to serve as your digital portfolio. You can then link your website in your bio to share more details about the project.

However, with so many social media platforms out there today, it is important to make sure you aren't wasting your time or spreading yourself too thin. I recommend focusing on the core platforms of Instagram, YouTube, and TikTok outside of your personal site or blog. I've never really gotten much out of Facebook, Twitter, Snapchat, and other platforms out there. You are better off mastering a few platforms versus having a weak presence on a dozen. Beyond that, you should keep an eye on trends. The big social media platform today is Instagram, but a decade ago it was Facebook. Five years before that, it was Myspace. Keep an eye on new and emerging social media platforms, as this could give you a similar first-mover advantage to the one that I had on YouTube in 2016.

What you are doing in this personal development phase of your life is setting yourself up for success. Spending a few months focusing on yourself may seem like a waste of time, but it could be the difference between sticking with your new side hustle and giving up and going back to life as it was before. Take the necessary time now to improve your skills and prepare for battle.

Key Takeaways

- Represent yourself and your business as professionally as possible. This, in turn, has an impact on how others perceive you and your business.

- Dressing well can help you feel more confident and motivated.

- The "keeping up with the Joneses" mentality is a financial trap. It becomes a game that nobody wins.

- Improve your skills with free information found online, such as YouTube videos.

- A consistent fitness routine is a great precursor to starting your own side hustle, as it teaches you the concept of discipline.

- Combat your bad habits early on. If your personal life is cluttered and disorganized, your business will be too.

- Take the time to establish a solid routine and schedule before adding a side hustle to the mix.

Be Prepared to Sacrifice

When it comes to starting your own side hustle, the number one thing you must be prepared for is sacrifice. Unfortunately, a lot of people try to start a side hustle at the wrong point of time in life. One of the best quotes I have heard related to this is "The worst time to start a business is when you need money." Most businesses do not make much money at all in the first few months of operations. In some cases, it could even take years to build something up. You should be prepared to sacrifice a tremendous amount of time, and potentially even money, to get it off the ground. Keep in mind that sacrificing money does not just mean sacrificing the investment you put into your business. It also means having to say no to other short-term opportunities that could make you money.

When I worked for the power utility company, there were many opportunities to work overtime at one and a half times normal pay or higher. I had to turn down a lot of this overtime because I knew that it would prevent me from being able to work on my channel. I had to say no to the prospect of earning money today in order to earn more money tomorrow. Most side hustles out there won't take a ton of money directly out of your bank account. However, you do have to consider the cost of potentially saying no to other opportunities. This ties in with one of the many important lessons that my parents taught me: every opportunity has a cost. You can't say yes to one thing without having to say no to other things. For me, it was an easy decision to make because I knew I had to eventually leave the utility company.

Become a "No" Person

Since every opportunity in life has a cost, you must be selective about the ones you say yes to in life. One of my favorite movies of all time is *Yes Man*. In this movie, Carl Allen (played by Jim Carrey) has to say yes to every opportunity that comes his way. It's a very funny premise, and it really helps him come out of his shell. However, your goal right now isn't to have a buzzing social life like Carl Allen. When starting a side hustle and focusing on yourself, you have to do the opposite and become a "no" person. You will probably find that you have to say "no" to things far more often than you say "yes." This simply comes down to your decision to focus on delayed gratification, while most others out there are focused on instant gratification. We currently live in a culture of "right now" where we want and expect everything to happen at the snap of our fingers. In a matter of minutes, we can now request a ride from our phone, order groceries, or even have food delivered from our favorite restaurant. If we are bored, there are countless apps on our phones offering an instant distraction from our current situation. And of course, there's always something new to watch on Netflix.

Something that I have always found interesting is that typically, the further you delay gratification, the better the outcome will be. Think about some of the most successful people in the world like Elon Musk and Jeff Bezos. For decades, these individuals have been focusing on delayed gratification through long-term goals. It can be difficult to reframe your mind to get excited about this delayed gratification, especially since everything else is so instantaneous. However, this is an essential step for long-term success with a side hustle that, like mine, could eventually become a full-blown business. According to *Forbes*, most new businesses do not even turn a profit in their first year of operations. Keep in mind that this statistic mostly applies to those who start a brick-and-mortar business like a restaurant. It is entirely possible to earn a profit from your side hustle within the first 12 months, or even sooner. This is largely based on the costs associated with getting each of these businesses off the ground. It costs a lot more money to start a restaurant versus a blog. With any business, you should have realistic expectations going in. When you first start your side hustle, you will essentially be working your butt off for free before you can start earning money.

Back when I started my YouTube channel, I was able to monetize it from day one. This meant that ads would be displayed before and alongside my videos, earning me a cut of the revenue generated. The very first month that I started doing YouTube videos, I made a grand total of $2.57 in ad revenue. At the time, I was spending about four hours a day working on my channel, roughly 30 hours a week. If you do the math, in October 2016, I spent around 120 hours working on my channel in order to earn $2.57 in total, meaning I was effectively working for $0.02 per hour. The following month, I ended up earning $7.16 in ad revenue. Most people would probably be discouraged by that, but I was actually very excited to see that my revenue had nearly tripled month over month. My thought process was that if this kept going, I would be making hundreds of dollars per month in no time at all.

In December 2016, I had two revenue streams. Alongside the ad revenue from my channel, I put together an e-book and started selling it for $14. I ended up selling two copies of the book, which earned me $28. In terms of the ad revenue, I made $31.99 that month. In total, that was $59.99 in revenue for the month of December 2016. You may think that is a lot of money for something that I just started. Or you might think that is an insignificant amount of money. Both are correct. It's certainly exciting to be able to pull money out of thin air on the internet, no matter what amount it may be. Keep in mind, though, most people would not be very excited about earning a total of $69.72 after spending hundreds of hours working on something. Not to mention, the ad revenue had to accrue to $100 before it could be paid out, so I hadn't actually received any money yet, except for my ebook sales. Despite this, I promised myself that I would not quit like I had many times in the past. History wasn't going to repeat itself. I had learned my lessons from starting and quitting over and over again, and I was determined to break the cycle.

You Don't Start a Business to Make Money

There is a misconception that a business is something you start when you are looking to make some money. It's as if people find themselves low on money and then ask themselves, "Should I start a business or go get a job?" I like to think of going out and getting a job as getting on a train that is already moving. Someone started this business a long time ago, and now they need people to operate it. The people who started this business took on a huge amount of risk initially, so now they have most of the potential success and earnings. It's very similar to what Warren Buffett said about sitting in the shade today because you planted a tree years ago. Starting a business is risky, there's no doubt about that. Certainly, there are things you can do to mitigate that risk, such as bootstrapping and working a job while side hustling. *Bootstrapping* is the concept of using what you have right now to get your business off the ground, even if you need the strap off of your own boots. However, you have to consider the risk and reward of any investment or opportunity out there. People who start a business take on a ton of stress and risk. If things go well, they may find themselves sitting in the shade years later while other people run the day-to-day operations. If things don't go well, they may have to start over and lick their wounds. That is simply the nature of business. The problem is, a lot of people want to be able to jump on a moving train, while also having the potential benefits of those who started the business. This is a classic situation of wishing to have your cake and eat it too.

If you want the opportunity for success that comes along with starting a business, you have to be comfortable with taking on the risk. Ask yourself: What risk is involved with going out and getting a job? There is practically zero risk. You simply apply for the position, send in a resume, and go to a job interview. In life, the potential "win" will almost always be proportional to the potential "loss" associated with the risk taken. That certainly doesn't mean you should go out and take the biggest risks possible. Sure, Elon Musk and Jeff Bezos are able to do this. But they are billionaires with tremendous amounts of resources at their disposal. Just remember that risk and reward are almost always proportional. The more you wager, the more you could win or lose.

I am a firm believer in working both a job and a side hustle simultaneously. It's entirely possible to do this; it just requires discipline and sacrifice, which is something a lot of people aren't comfortable with. Early on, with any side hustle, you need to find some motivating force to keep you going outside of earning money. In fact, you shouldn't even be thinking about making money at first. This is where your "why" should come into play. When you start a side hustle with the goal of simply making money, you aren't focused on the right thing, which is providing value to others.

I started my YouTube channel because I felt like I wasn't making a difference in the world. Sure, eventually I hoped to make money from it. However, initially my focus was to help people. Before I became disengaged from school during my teenage years, I was a total teacher's pet in elementary school. My teachers were my heroes, and as a kid, I wanted to be a teacher because of the many of the amazing teachers I had in school. I was able to fulfill this by educating others on YouTube instead of in a traditional classroom setting. Later, I started the Investing Simple blog with a similar goal in mind. We wanted to provide simple and easy-to-read comparison and review content for the myriad of investing apps available today, "no finance degree required."

Many people do not take the time to lay the proper foundation for a business. Instead, they try to force motivation by quitting their job. Some foolishly think that removing the safety net of stable income will force them to succeed. "Burn the bridges," as they say. Well, I'm here to tell you to put the matches down. I have yet to see this pan out well for anyone. Putting that much pressure on yourself to make money is a surefire way to set yourself up for bad decision-making. Unfortunately, a lot of people out there are looking for some type of hack or shortcut to success. Even though people all over the internet claim to have hacks for success, I can tell you right now that is not the case. There are no shortcuts, only strategies, and trying to force motivation will end in disaster. Focusing on making money from a business as an immediate goal will also end in disaster. Remember that money is simply a by-product of value being provided in some form. I have seen many people start a business with the goal of making money immediately, and I've yet to see it work out well.

Your Friends, Family, Relationships, and Pets

When you are starting a new venture, the two most important resources you have are your time and money. The time aspect is typically far more important, as there are many side hustles you can start today with minimal capital investment. As a result, you must pay very close attention to the things consuming both your time and your money. One of the most common questions I get from people is whether you can be in a relationship while working a job and starting your hustle on the side. My answer has always been that it depends on what type of relationship you are in. If you are not in a relationship right now, the answer is flat out no. You should not be actively pursuing a relationship while starting a business, working a day job, and focusing on your own personal development. These days, finding a relationship is a very time-consuming process. It's practically a side hustle in and of itself. Even using a dating app takes hours of time that could instead be spent on your side hustle. You cannot afford to squander your time like this. If you are currently in a relationship, you will have to clearly communicate your plans and goals with your partner. Hopefully, your partner understands and supports your decision. If not, you may need to consider whether this relationship is the best thing for you at this time. The right relationship can help you as you pursue your dreams and build your own business. The wrong relationship can be a huge consumer of your time, energy, and money.

Moving on from relationships, the next thing to consider is pets. I personally have five pets: three small cats and two small dogs. While these pets are a great addition to my life in most cases, they can also be a huge consumer of both time and money. For that reason, I would not recommend going out and getting a new pet while trying to start a business. Having a kitten or a puppy is a lot of work, not to mention the frequent and costly trips to the vet. This is probably not the time to add that into your life. If you already have pets, you may need to spend some time training them before you start devoting a lot of time to your new business venture. For example, if your dog barks around the clock, that will become a huge distraction for you. You are better off taking the time to create a good solution, even if that delays the start of your new side hustle. Maybe you find that taking your dog for a 20-minute walk eliminates this barking. That should then be something you incorporate as part of your daily routine.

Let me give you an example of this from my own life. Having three cats can definitely be a handful, and one of the biggest annoyances for me is cat litter getting every-where. When we got our third cat, I was getting into a lot of arguments with my fiancée over the litter problem. I was vacuuming around the litter boxes three to five times a day, and this was becoming a huge time suck for me. Not only that, but every time I had to vacuum, I got completely derailed from whatever I was currently working on. After a few weeks of this, I realized that I needed to come up with a better solution. To solve this problem creatively, we ended up getting a litter box that is specifically designed to reduce mess. Now we vacuum only once a day. It is well worth it to take the time to figure out these systems and solutions for the small annoyances in your life. It took about the same amount of time I spent vacuuming to research and order this new litter box online. This new litter box has allowed me to reclaim at least 30 minutes a day in addition to cutting down on interruptions and arguments.

What about the people in your life? One of the best pieces of advice I was ever given was to pay attention to how I felt emotionally after hanging out with someone. If you feel tired, unmotivated, or drained after spending time with someone, that person is an "energy vampire." You should be surrounding yourself with people who leave you feeling motivated and driven. When I started out with the self-improvement phase of my life, I tried to continue the same ongoing friendships. However, this was very difficult because many of the things my friends wanted to do didn't align with my goals at the time. For example, they would usually want to go out to a bar and grab a beer. While that was something I would do regularly in the past (and something I do now), I realized that doing so was no longer serving me at that time. I was dedicated to working on my channel in the evening, and I didn't want to drink a beer and get tired. This made socializing difficult and eventually led to a three-month period during which I didn't see much of my friends or drink alcohol.

I realized I felt unmotivated after hanging out with my friends. I couldn't talk to them about my dreams and aspirations, as they didn't fully understand what I was doing. Instead, like most others, my friends were looking for instant gratification in the form of a cold beer. So I minimized my "circle of influence" to a select few for a period of time. Positive energy is an important resource that you need to preserve, and you have to be very mindful of the people and things that take this away from you. I encourage you to do an audit of the people in your life to identify who lifts you up and who leaves you feeling drained. Unfortunately, you can't control some of the people you spend time around, like coworkers. However, you have complete control over who you spend time with outside of work.

Most of your friends and family members are probably working to make money, not necessarily to do what they love. I'd also say it's a safe bet to assume most of them work in regular 9-to-5 jobs. Keep in mind that it's human nature for others around you to want to keep you on their level. If all your friends are simply working jobs and drinking beer, that's exactly what they want you to be doing too. As soon as they see you going off and doing something different, they may criticize you. The basic concept at play here is "misery loves company." If everyone is stuck in the same bad situation together, there is a collective sense of hopelessness. As soon as someone shatters that veil of hopelessness by going out and trying something new, others will be bothered. However, some may support you, and you should make note of who these people are. This is your most important support network: those who want to see you reach your fullest potential regardless of where it leaves them.

You may want to prepare to take some space from those who do not support you. I spent a lot of time deepening relationships with those who did support my vision, such as my mom and my mentor, Jake. (I'll discuss this mentorship in Lesson 7.) During this time in your life, don't be afraid to take a break and disconnect like I did. You can always rekindle old friendships later on. Or you might find some people weren't the best addition to your life in the first place. One good way to do this is to tell your friends you are focusing on yourself and going through a personal development phase. It's hard enough to start a side hustle without having people criticize you and tear you down. Like me, you will probably find out who your real friends are by seeing who understands and supports you. Who knows, you may even inspire them to go out and start a side hustle of their own.

Eliminate Phone Distractions

The next area of your life that you need to sacrifice is time spent on your phone. Going back to our discussion on instant gratification, that's basically exactly what your phone offers you at all times of the day. You are probably spending a lot of time on your phone throughout the day, whether you're texting friends, catching up on the news, playing games, or checking the stocks. This is a bad habit that you are going to have to break. Here's how:

- **Delete any apps that are not currently serving your purpose.** Sorry, that's going to include

Tinder and your other dating apps. In addition, if you have any games on your phone, you need to delete them. Most phones today have a feature that allows you to see what apps you spend the most time using. Go through that list and delete the apps that cause you to waste time.

- **Turn off the notifications for the rest of the apps on your phone.** You don't have to turn off notifications for every single app. For example, I leave notifications on for apps like Venmo and other money/banking apps. These are rarely the problem. Simply go into the settings on your phone and turn off all of these unnecessary notifications for nonessential apps.

- **Turn off your ringer, at least during your work time.** According to a study done by the University of California, on average it takes about 23 minutes to get back on task after a distraction. To avoid this, I leave my phone completely out of the room when I am working.

- **Decide on a time interval during which you can check your phone.** Since you now know how problematic distractions are in terms of focus, you should aim to only check your phone in between tasks. Instead of having the phone tell you when it is time to check it, only check your phone when it is a good time for you. The ideal time would be when you finish a task.

There are going to be some exceptions here. For example, parents reading this will probably have to leave their ringer on in case things happen, such as the school calling. In this case, I recommend only enabling the ringer for specific contacts. This is easy to set up in your phone settings. You may also find that you need to talk to friends and family members about how often they are texting you, and in how much detail. Something I have always struggled with is feeling like I need to respond to every single text I get within a short period of time. You really don't have to do this, and responding less frequently will actually cut down on the number of texts you receive.

Vacation and Sick Time

Another area that I sacrificed is how I used my vacation time and sick days while working for the power company. If you don't follow exactly what I did here, it's not the end of the world. Taking a break from everything and letting your mind rest for a period of time can be one of the most beneficial things you can do. Personally, at the time I didn't really see value in spending money and using my vacation time to actually go on a vacation. While I did take a few trips with my mom and brother during the time that I was working a job, I used the majority of my sick and vacation time to instead work on my business. I knew that I eventually wanted the freedom to go to the beach or travel somewhere exciting whenever I wanted to, so I used all of the resources I had available to work toward that eventual long-term goal. I wanted my entire life to be that vacation, in a way, and I was prepared to do anything to make that happen. That may seem like an unattainable goal, but it is very much possible today. With the growth of remote work, it's possible to get your work done wherever there is Wi-Fi.

It takes a lot of determination, motivation, and willpower to sacrifice correctly. You have to shift your entire life from instant gratification to delayed gratification, almost fully living for tomorrow. Despite the name "side hustle," you can't just focus on it on the side and expect to have success. Your side hustle really has to be in the back of your mind 24/7, dictating almost every action and decision you make in life. For a period of time at least, it has to be the single most important thing to you.

Key Takeaways

- Recognize that building a successful side hustle involves turning down other short-term moneymaking opportunities.

- Become a "no" person. Be very careful about how you spend both your time and your money; these are your resources for success.

- In most cases, the further you delay gratification, the better the outcome will be.

- Risk and reward are almost always proportional. You can't have a massive upside without taking on the proportional risk or downside.

- Starting a side hustle with the goal of making money is a bad strategy. Instead, focus on providing value to others. Money is simply a by-product of value being provided.

- The right relationships can help you pursue your dreams and build your business. Focus on the relationships that lift you up, not the ones that bring you down.

- Eliminate as many distractions from your life as possible. You cannot afford to waste time.

Follow the Golden Rule

During a particularly slow night at JCPenney, my coworker told me about the company history. It had been incorporated in 1913 by a man named James Cash Penney. In 1898, Penney was working for a small chain of stores called the Golden Rule. The stores were based on the simple premise of treating others the way you would want to be treated. In a store setting, this meant top-notch customer service that was second to none. At the time, the Golden Rule was owned by two partners. The partners were impressed by Penney's work ethic and brought him on as a third partner. The trio opened a few more Golden Rule stores, but in 1907, the two original owners decided to dissolve their partnership. James Cash Penney bought them out, purchasing full interest in the stores. In 1913, the company was incorporated under a new name: J.C. Penney Company.

Decades later, JCPenney's approach to customer service was still based on that original principle. At the store, we were taught to put customer service above all else, even if it meant spending a lot of time attending to one customer's needs. Even though JCPenney is a shadow of its former self today, there is something to be said about being in business for over a century. The legacy of the company is a direct result of the values instilled by James Cash Penney, the two original partners of the Golden Rule, and other JCPenney leaders over time. If you want long-term business success, which you should, you need to choose a value system to follow. Just as JCPenney was founded on the principle of the Golden Rule, you too need to choose your core values carefully. If you don't choose a value system to follow, one will choose you, and it may not be the right one. It's similar to having no plan after high school. You are still going to end up doing something, so why not have a say in what that is?

It is certainly possible to have some level of success by following dishonest practices and taking advantage of others. However, this rarely results in any kind of sustained outcome. You are far better off sticking to your core values. I have always found that focusing on earning more money in the future, or delayed gratification, is the way to go. Someone who is looking to sell the most expensive product or whatever earns them the most money is looking for instant gratification. They aren't thinking about customer relationships down the line; their goal is to make as much money as they can today. Over time, they will find that they are sacrificing their integrity by doing this. Customers will realize that they weren't sold the best product or service, so they won't return or recommend the business to others.

The Principles of the Golden Rule

Using the Golden Rule as a springboard, I've brainstormed my own unique set of principles that can be applied to both business and everyday life. This value system has allowed me to have sustained success across multiple businesses. I have found that following these principles builds an immense amount of trust between you and your customers, which correspondingly generates revenue. I encourage you to follow these principles within your own life and business.

1. DON'T RECOMMEND THINGS YOU DON'T BELIEVE IN YOURSELF.

Let me start by asking you a simple question: If you had pizza that was burnt, tasteless, or just plain bad at a restaurant, would you recommend that restaurant to a friend? Of course not! But what if that restaurant offered you $10 for every new customer you referred? That shouldn't change your answer.

Yet there are some out there who would be willing to recommend the bad pizza to make a few bucks. If you loved this restaurant, most would say that it is fair game to profit from a genuine tip. Most of the money earned from my blogs comes from recommendations just like this.

However, instead of pizza, I recommend digital products like investment apps.

In my opinion, there is nothing wrong with earning a commission based on genuine and authentic recommendations. My YouTube subscribers continue to follow my channel and videos because they know that they can trust me. I am very transparent about my revenue streams, so my audience is fully aware that I am compensated by my affiliate partners. You too can help others by only providing recommendations for products and services you believe in. In addition, providing good recommendations increases the likelihood of repeat business and referrals.

2. DISCLOSE YOUR FINANCIAL INTERESTS.

Transparency is one of my core business values. Since the internet is such an anonymous place, I try to be as forthcoming as possible with my audience to win over and maintain their trust. While this has meant posting videos about five-figure stock losses in the past, it also means being as transparent as possible about my revenue streams from different online resources.

This goes above and beyond just following the Golden Rule. You have a legal obligation to make certain disclosures per the Federal Trade Commission (FTC). Disclosing your financial interests will help build trust with your audience and will keep you on the right side of the law. You should consult with a professional about the specifics of your disclaimer needs, but for now just keep the overall concept in mind.

As a general rule of thumb, if you are compensated in any way, you need to disclose this to your audience. Compensation doesn't just mean receiving money either. Something as simple as a company sending you free products in exchange for a social media review can also be considered compensation. Per the FTC, you would be required to disclose the value of the items received to your audience alongside your review.

While this might make you nervous, it's not hard to stay in compliance with these rules. Most of it is just common sense. I always have leaned toward over-disclaiming whenever possible. For example, if I mention a stock in a video, I will always disclose if I have holdings of that company.

3. REPRESENT YOURSELF HONESTLY.

In Lesson 2, we talked about the concept of perception and how this can be used to your advantage. While this principle may seem to contradict that, I think there is room for both. I believe it is possible to represent yourself honestly while using what you have to your advantage to build up your public persona. When I first began recording videos for my channel, I would put on my nice watch and dress shirts to make myself appear more professional. This, in turn, encouraged people to listen to what I had to say. Through my content, I built rapport by representing myself both professionally and honestly. I didn't lie to people about having a background in finance or anything like that. I authentically represented myself as an average guy on the internet, just one who dressed and carried himself well.

Beyond just your financial interests, it is vital to be honest with people about your knowledge of a given subject. To be an effective salesperson, you need to completely understand the product or service that you are selling. I spend many hours testing out different investing apps on my phone before creating content about them. Although time-consuming, this allows me to gain knowledge about what I am discussing or recommending. You don't need to be an expert to talk about most things online. But if you are not an expert on a certain topic, you should be transparent about your status as a "novice" or "beginner." For example, if you review an app you just downloaded, you could mention that your comments are based on your first impression of the product. Doing so gives your audience realistic expectations about your understanding of the subject matter. This may lead them to seek out additional resources before making a final decision, which may not be a bad idea.

Before I started posting videos on YouTube, I had a lot of limiting beliefs. One of them was that I was not credible enough to make videos educating others online. Since I don't have a formal background in finance, I felt that people would simply not listen to me. I ended up learning that there are many different types of experts out there. In fact, being a novice at something can be a benefit, depending on the circumstances. At this point, I've been making videos and writing about different financial topics for over half a decade, and I've become out of touch with a lot of the hurdles beginner investors face early on because I went through that phase so long ago. In many ways, a beginner investor documenting their experience would be able to better understand the pain points that their audience would be going through. Simply put, you do not need to be an expert at a subject in order to create content about it, as long as you are transparent about your level of knowledge. In fact, being a beginner can come with advantages that allow you to better serve those who are just getting started with something.

You also have a legal obligation to represent yourself honestly. Since I am providing content about finance, I am especially careful to represent myself accurately. If I lied to my audience and told them I was a financial advisor, I could get in big trouble. This legal obligation also extends to other niches. There could also be legal consequences if you misrepresent yourself as a doctor, a dietician, or any professional providing medical or legal advice.

4. VALUE REPEAT BUSINESS OVER MAKING A SALE.

At JCPenney, this was the most prevalent embodiment of the Golden Rule that I saw on a day-to-day basis. We were never pushed to reach any kind of sales target, or to make sure every customer left with a bag in hand. Instead, JCPenney was an environment where staff felt comfortable to give authentic recommendations, even if that meant not making a sale that day. There were a few competing

department stores near the JCPenney where I worked.
When people asked about comparing prices with those
other stores, I would encourage them to do so. Those
same people would often come back later that day, seek me
out, and tell me that our jackets were either cheaper or of
better quality.

You may be eager to start making money, but that is no
excuse to violate the Golden Rule. Keep in mind, your
business should prioritize helping others and providing
value to your customers rather than making money.
Money is simply the by-product. As a result, you need to
be prepared to delay gratification when necessary. For
example, if you have a wine shop and find that your store
doesn't carry a specific wine a customer is looking for, you
are better off telling them where they can get it instead of
trying to sell them something else. The next time they are
looking for a different wine, maybe something less specific,
they might think back to the positive experience they had
with you and come back in. These interactions build trust
and rapport, which often leads to repeat business and
referrals. Always value repeat business over an immediate
sale right now, delayed gratification over instant gratification. Think about the lifetime value of a customer versus
the value of a one-time sale.

5. OFFER SUPPORT TOOLS.
This ties in with the idea of adding value first. Instead
of just offering information about the product or service,
teach your customer how to use it. As the competition

increased on YouTube, I had to figure out ways to provide more value to my audience. Whereas before I was just making short videos, I now had to create longer, step-by-step guides and tutorials to outrank others with similar content. This was helping me get more views and subscribers, but I needed to ensure that people were using my affiliate links too. At the end of the day, there was no differentiating factor between my link and someone else's link.

After putting some thought into this and having discussions with my peers, I learned about something called a "bridge page." This term can be used for a number of different applications. In my case, it meant connecting or "bridging" the gap between my audience and the affiliate offer. In practice, I provided my audience with a freebie in exchange for signing up with my affiliate link. There's no way to make sure that someone uses your link—it remains totally optional. However, what I have found is that most people are more than willing to use your affiliate link after you provide them with something of high value. This can be accomplished in the "real world" too. Providing customers with free lessons in-store or pamphlets about how to use the items you sell accomplishes the same goal. An example of how I provide support tools digitally is a free course I made about online course creation on Teachable, a course creation platform. (You can find it on my website, ryanoscribner.com.) I spent a few weeks putting together dozens of lessons teaching the ins and outs of creating and launching your own online course or membership site. I am affiliated with Teachable, so I earn a recurring commission when people sign up via my link. Instead of simply trying to get people to sign up for Teachable, my course shows them how to build their own course step by step.

Since Teachable is a monthly subscription, the commission earned on the sale is recurring as well. By teaching my students "how to fish," or create a course/membership site themselves, they have a better chance of success. If they are having success and making money, they will keep their Teachable subscription and I'll keep earning my monthly commission.

By offering free guides, trainings, and courses through bridge pages, I have been able to remain competitive in the affiliate marketing space on YouTube. This has also become a clear differentiating factor between my channel and other channels that compete with me. As a result, many others have followed suit and created free training bridge pages and offers. Once you are generating high volume for your affiliate, you can reach out to them and ask if they can provide you with a unique sign-up incentive for your audience.

6. AVOID NEGATIVE CAMPAIGNING.

Through my mom's journalism career, I met a lot of interesting people over the years. Many of these people were involved in politics in some form. My mom covered a lot of local meetings in the news, so she would have conversations with mayors, supervisors, and other local officials. While I haven't made a formal decision about getting into politics in the future, I have learned countless lessons from my political connections. In terms of the Golden Rule, the most important lesson for me is steering clear of negative campaigning—the practice of intentionally spreading negative information about someone to influence the public's perception of that individual. I spent a lot of time with John Romano, the former mayor of my small hometown. In the two and a half decades he served us, he never once deployed negative campaigning strategies. His opponents would, however. Nonetheless, he was reelected every single term until he retired at his own will.

Bringing this back to content creation, there are countless platforms out there that solely rely on this "negative campaigning" strategy to garner attention online. Like my friend John, the former mayor, I made the decision a long time ago to avoid this strategy. It's certainly entertaining to watch channels out there such as Coffeezilla that expose different shady characters and scams. However, this does come with significant risks, the main one being the target it puts on your back. Stephen from the channel Coffeezilla has been hit with multiple cease-and-desist lawsuits over the years based on his videos about others. It is also important to consider your overall safety, as speaking poorly of others with deep pockets can be outright dangerous. For safety, legality, and many other reasons, I recommend avoiding any negative remarks about others.

That's not to say that there isn't a real need for this type of investigative journalism and reporting in society. In fact, a lot of criminal or unethical activities are uncovered through a local news investigation. Like the saying attributed to George Orwell, "Journalism is printing what someone else does not want printed; everything else is public relations." The important difference here is working for a news publication that has a legal counsel and follows set investigative procedures, versus going out and doing it on your own. My recommendation is to steer clear of this investigative style of content, despite its importance.

What Is Affiliate Marketing?

Since this is the cornerstone of most of my businesses, I think it's important to cover the basics of affiliate marketing. The concept is relatively straightforward. We all make recommendations to people in our lives about our favorite products and services. Affiliate marketing simply enables you to get paid for your recommendations.

When you become an affiliate for a given product or service, you get your own unique tracking link to share with your audience. When someone clicks on that link, a tracking cookie is activated. This is a type of coding in the back end of the website that allows the lead to be tracked and attributed to you, the affiliate. Each affiliate has a different cookie duration, which is the period of time that the lead is attributed to you—for example, 30 days or six months. If that lead ends up signing up for the service or purchasing the product within that cookie duration, you as the affiliate earn a commission from the sale. The amount earned varies per brand, and it can change over time. A lot of brands will pay you more based on the volume of referrals you bring in. The more you send them, the more you earn per lead. The action being tracked differs as well. Sometimes, it is simply signing up for an email list. In other cases, the referral may need to make a purchase or a deposit in order for you to earn your commission.

I got into affiliate marketing with my YouTube channel through the Amazon Associates program. This is one of the largest and most popular affiliate programs out there today. The program allows you to earn a commission by referring sales over to Amazon. Initially, I decided to put links to my favorite books as well as my recording equipment in the descriptions of all my YouTube videos. I was getting a lot of questions from my audience about my book recommendations and the gear I used to record my videos. I figured this was a good way to answer those questions and earn a little extra money in the process.

With the Amazon Associates program, the percentage commission that you earn varies depending on the product category. These commission rates change often, so I won't go into specific detail here. You can simply Google search for "Amazon Associates commission rates" to see the current percentages yourself; they tend to range from a 1 percent commission all the way up to 10 percent or more. I first started placing Amazon affiliate links in my video descriptions in June 2017 and was very pleased when I ended up making $31.34 that month. To be able to have money appear out of thin air by simply placing links on my content was a fascinating concept. This revenue stream grew quite a bit to $146.05 in July. To my surprise, most of the products I was earning commissions on were not the ones I was linking to in the descriptions of my videos. I was earning commissions on some pretty strange products, such as outdoor lizard repellent.

I learned that the tracking cookie associated with Amazon Associates lasts for 24 hours, and it doesn't matter what the person buys during the time frame—I earn a commission. Someone could click on a link in my description for a book, close Amazon, open it again 23 hours later and purchase something completely different, and I would still earn a commission. One of the wildest examples of this was a high-end vacuum cleaner someone purchased after clicking on one of my links. The vacuum cleaner was around $1,500 and was in an 8 percent commission category at the time. I ended up earning a commission of around $120 just from that one sale.

The Business Model of Affiliate Marketing

The first thing I came to appreciate about the business model of affiliate marketing is how passive it is. After learning important lessons from *Rich Dad, Poor Dad* by Robert Kiyosaki, I knew I needed to be able to make money 24/7, ideally in a passive manner, instead of only earning money during work hours, in an active manner. This fact alone makes the business model of affiliate marketing very scalable. My content is always available online—someone can watch one of my videos on the other side of the world while I'm asleep, and I can make money during that window of time.

Imagine if you were to sell your own product. Sure, you might be able to make more money than you would as an affiliate. However, this would now shift from a very passive income stream to a very active one. All tasks related to customer acquisition, or the work involved with bringing in a new customer, would now fall on your shoulders. Some examples of this include ongoing email marketing or running retargeting ads on social media. Beyond that, you would also be responsible for managing order fulfillment as well as handling any complaints and potential returns. In addition, you would be fully responsible for customer service as well. This business model is difficult to scale. If you wanted to go from selling 10 products a week to 500, you would have to create more systems and possibly hire someone to manage order fulfillment. In addition, the number of returns and complaints you would receive would scale at a similar rate. If you average one complaint per 25 orders, you should expect around 10 complaints on 250 orders.

As an affiliate marketer, it doesn't matter if one person clicks on your link or 10,000 people in terms of the work involved. All of the leg work is handled by your affiliate. You don't have to worry about your email inbox blowing up with customer service–related questions or complaints. Not to mention, you are able to leverage all of the systems created by your affiliate. Most of the companies involved with affiliate marketing today will have great systems set up, such as email marketing sequences and social media retargeting ads. In most cases, that sale is still attributed back to you, even if your lead doesn't sign up immediately and registers after clicking on a retargeting social media ad later. Even though the company is spending additional money on ads, you would still earn your full commission, assuming the conversion or sale took place within your cookie duration window.

One caveat here is that you may want to answer questions your audience has about something before they commit. While this is optional, I have found that it significantly increases conversions. For example, if someone asked me what the minimum investment was on M1 Finance in an Instagram DM, I will absolutely respond to them. You should also check for questions like this within the comments of your content posted online.

Email autoresponders are often a very powerful part of this process as well. For example, I'm affiliated with a crowdfunded real estate investment platform called Fundrise. With this particular affiliate, the landing page is an email drop where my lead simply has to give them their name and email to learn more about the investment. If someone clicks on my link and signs up for the email list, the tracking window for the conversion is several months. During that time period, the affiliate will be sending marketing emails through an automated sequence. If they eventually open one of those emails and decide to invest, that conversion is attributed to me.

Eventually, I decided to take this a step further by creating my own autoresponder sequences. I have always closely followed what others are doing around me and have done my best to duplicate the strategies. After seeing the success Fundrise was having with this autoresponder, I made my own email sequences for my different affiliate bridge offers. For example, if you sign up for my free e-book on real estate crowdfunding, you will automatically receive a series of emails related to Fundrise after the guide is sent over to you. This is done with no human involvement, making the activity completely passive. You can do well as an affiliate marketer by simply placing links within your content. If you want to do exceptionally well, you have to deploy these more advanced affiliate marketing strategies.

Unethical Affiliate Marketing

Remember when I mentioned recommending bad pizza to earn a few bucks? Over the years, I've met people firsthand who would probably do that. Let me give you an example. At one point in time, I discussed a fitness routine I was doing with a friend who also had an online following. I was working out consistently and following a high-protein diet, so I ended up getting in really good shape in a short period of time. After hearing about this, my friend recommended that I find a supplement or fitness training to become affiliated with. Then, he suggested sending an email to my audience with before and after photos, with a link to the affiliate offer. I was very taken aback by what my friend suggested because it was rooted in dishonesty. I had gotten into shape by following an exercise routine and a high-protein diet, not because of some random program or supplement online. If I were to make an honest video about my process and included affiliate links for the protein power I used, that would be ethical because I would be sharing exactly what I used and what worked for me. If I instead sent an email out to my audience linking to a high-commission weight-loss supplement, the results would be mixed at best. Clearly, I would be breaking many of my principles of the Golden Rule. I would not be recommending something that I believed in or was even familiar with. Those who followed my advice would soon realize they had been misled, and they would be unlikely to return to me for a future recommendation of any kind.

A lot of people become completely detached from the fact that real people interact with their content and follow their advice. Intentionally misleading them to earn a high commission is certainly nothing to be proud of. I often refer to my affiliate links as a "community tip jar," where people can give back to me at no additional cost to them if they wish to do so. Countless times now, I have received comments from people about how they specifically used my link because I was honest with them about the affiliate relationship. The idea behind affiliate marketing isn't to generate random commissions by misleading strangers on the internet. Instead, it is to build trust with your audience and give them genuine recommendations based on what has worked well for you or others. If you wouldn't recommend it to a friend, don't recommend it to a stranger online just because it's anonymous. What if you were the one being misled by someone on the internet? Think back to the Golden Rule. People are always going to be naturally suspicious about things, especially online. If they see you mentioning the same product, brand, or company repeatedly, they will suspect you have some type of relationship with them. Disclose, disclose, disclose. This is how you build trust and rapport.

When I began exploring options for making money online, I realized there was a certain level of anonymity and detachment associated with providing services to others on the internet. It was not the same as helping customers find a nice shirt and tie for a job interview like I had done countless times before. Unfortunately, because the internet is a largely anonymous realm, there are many out there operating businesses that do not follow any of the principles of the Golden Rule. However, if you want to have sustained success, it is imperative that you follow them.

In a traditional brick-and-mortar retail environment, you are right there in person with your customers. As a result, you are far more likely to follow principles of the Golden Rule because you are likely to see your customers again. Even if they don't come back into your store, you might run into them if they live in the area. In addition, they know exactly where to find you should they have a bad experience with your product or service. The online business setting is completely different. In this scenario, your customers are numbers in an analytics dashboard. You do not interact with them directly; it is a far more detached experience without personal interaction. This, unfortunately, leads some to forget that they are even interacting with real people. Instead, it all becomes about the numbers.

JCPenney didn't have a specific set of guidelines that we had to follow. Instead, they made us feel comfortable with providing the best possible service to the customers, thus deploying the Golden Rule. It was all about the customer. Whatever they needed, if we could do it, we would. On one occasion, this meant pulling out the fabric steamer used for the mannequins to steam a shirt for a customer on the way to an important event.

Although the online world is a less personal environment, I challenge you to find ways to go above and beyond for your audience. Every number on the analytics dashboard is a real person, and they are trusting you to guide them to the right place.

Key Takeaways

- Follow the Golden Rule: treat others the way you would like to be treated. The Golden Rule allows you to put yourself in the shoes of the people you are helping.

- Always value repeat business over an immediate sale—delayed gratification over instant gratification.

- Instead of simply offering information about a product or service, teach your customer how to use it. In return, you are likely to be rewarded with referrals and repeat business.

- Following the Golden Rule will build trust with your customers. That trust will, in turn, generate revenue.

- We all make recommendations to people in our lives about different products and services. Affiliate marketing allows you to get paid for making recommendations.

- Don't become detached from the real people you are helping and interacting with online. It's easy to forget this and become caught up in the numbers.

- Stick to focusing on the positives, not the negatives. Negative campaigning, or spreading information to tarnish someone's image, opens the door for others to do the same to you.

Frugality 101

Our thoughts, feelings, and habits surrounding money are often rooted in our childhood experiences. As we grew up watching our parents or other adults around us, many of us learned to view money as a medium of exchange. This simply means primarily using money to obtain the resources or necessities that we needed and, if we were lucky, some of our wants or desires as well.

At certain points, my household was operating paycheck to paycheck, something I wasn't aware of until years later. When I was growing up, my mom worked from home as a freelance journalist for local newspapers, but her income was rather sporadic. (Years later, this field has just about disappeared.) My dad worked as a branch manager for several different banks before eventually transitioning into a financial advisor when I was a bit older.

For many reasons, my parents were never able to build up a lot of assets outside of equity in their home. At one point, my dad did own a rental property, though he had to sell after a string of bad tenants caused damage. (One woman did not disclose that she had three ferrets running loose in the house. My dad had to spend thousands replacing the carpet and painting the walls due to the damage they caused.) Before my parents got divorced, my siblings and I had a typical middle-class life in the suburbs. We certainly weren't rich, but there was never a shortage of presents under the tree on Christmas either. In addition, we took trips to the beach in Maine every summer, even the year my dad got laid off. He spent the entire trip in bed. I didn't understand why he was so upset, but as an adult now, I cannot imagine the fear of losing your income when you have a household and a family to support. My parents, like most, ended up using money mostly as a medium of exchange for things like groceries, clothes, and a few extras here and there.

In my teens, I also used money as a medium of exchange. The day I turned 16, I got my driver's permit and ended up getting my own car with some help from my grandfather. He had set aside $5,000 for each of his grandchildren to buy their first vehicle, which helped us out tremendously. Most of the money I earned from my job at JCPenney went toward gas and insurance for my car, which ended up being quite expensive. On a few occasions, I found myself paying for gas with the loose change in my cupholder. However, it was all worth it to me to have my freedom. I was the only one in my group of friends with a car, so I was the go-to for transport. It gave me a "cool" edge.

I had a major paradigm shift in terms of how I viewed money during my first semester of college. Instead of just spending it, I began viewing money as a resource that could buy back my time too. I had spent the previous summer working nearly full-time at JCPenney, so I had saved up a few thousand dollars. One day, I sat down at lunch, mapped out my expenses, and concluded that I had enough money to make it through the entire semester without working. So I made the decision to leave that job. For the first time, I decided to use money to buy freedom. My plan was to pick up a holiday job during the month-long winter break before the second semester. As a result, I was able to fully devote myself to my studies and I really kicked butt in college. I was also able to take time to enjoy myself and hang out with friends on weekends. Before this, I viewed money as means to pay for the things I wanted or needed in my life. However, this changed as I began to see money as a fuel source that needed to be monitored and conserved as much as possible, not just spent frivolously. I shifted from using money to purchase things to carefully budgeting and doling only what I needed to sustain myself. Once you shift your viewpoint to think of money as a fuel source and not just a medium of exchange, you become far more selective about how you use this fuel.

You are always going to use some percentage of your income as a medium of exchange. At the end of the day, that is what money was created for. You have a lot of control over spending on your wants, but you also have control on spending related to your needs as well. I learned this firsthand with my mom when I was 16. At the time, my brother and I were living in the house she was renting for us across town from where I grew up. Based on my mom's income, we qualified for food stamps. It wasn't much, but I helped my mom make the most of it through the use of coupons and savvy shopping habits. For example, toilet paper is something that we would all deem as an essential. However, we all pay different prices for it based on where we buy it and, you know, "preference." While I won't get into a two-ply versus one-ply discussion, it is worth considering where you are buying things. Are you paying three dollars a roll by purchasing a four-pack at the gas station once a week? Or are you paying one dollar a roll by buying it in bulk online? These cost savings on your "needs" allow you to minimize the amount of money you are using as a medium of exchange.

Using Your Fuel Source Properly

I was fortunate enough to experience this shift in mindset during my early twenties, but not everyone comes to this realization. As people make more money, they usually spend more money on the things they want. This is referred to as "lifestyle inflation." While working for the utility company, I was amazed at how prevalent lifestyle inflation was. During the month of April, the buzz around the office was about how each person was going to spend their tax refund and company bonus, since both came around the same time. When asked about my plan, I told my peers I planned on investing my money. They told me I was "boring," since I wasn't going to blow the cash on a new ATV like some of them planned on doing.

There are many problems with lifestyle inflation, but the biggest tends to be that it entraps you. As your lifestyle inflates, it is going to become more and more expensive to maintain. When this happens, you have to work harder to earn more money. Typically, this means saying yes to a lot of overtime or going out and getting a second or third job. While I did work the occasional overtime shift for storms, I said no to almost every opportunity to work extra hours. I needed to say no in order to have time to focus on my side hustle, but my decision to save rather than splurge is what allowed me to be able to say no. Lifestyle inflation puts you in a position where you cannot say no. You can't afford to do so. Keep in mind that this lifestyle inflation is often a result of caring about the wrong form of perception. It doesn't matter what your coworkers think, especially if you are trying to escape like me.

It didn't take me long to realize that I would not be able to stay at the utility company for my entire life, let alone another year. As a result, I realized that I needed to build up a significant fuel reserve of money in order to transition into my own business venture. I ended up referring to this as my "freedom fund." This freedom fund would serve as my allocation of money to live on and would give me the freedom to leave my unsatisfying job and scale my YouTube channel. By living off the fuel of my savings instead of my wages, as I had during college, I could spend my time building up my business. By the time I quit my job, I had $30,000 in savings as well as some different investments in the stock market.

Despite having a lot of funds, I didn't want to put all my assets at risk while trying to get my side hustle off the ground. Instead, I took $5,000 and put this in a separate bank account for living expenses. This would be my fuel reserve that I would use to get my time back. I promised myself that if I ran out of the $5,000 freedom fund, I would simply go out and get another job. I was not going to allow myself to use up my entire fuel source on this one idea. I didn't want to risk two years of savings, which could potentially leave me back at square one. If you too decide to take a leap of faith, I'd recommend a similar strategy. Simply put, it's never a good idea to put all of your eggs in one basket. You might even decide to split your "freedom fund" in half, with the plan of switching gears if the first idea is not taking off. Keep in mind, it's rare to have success with the first side hustle you try. I had proof of concept with mine, but I still didn't want to go all in with it financially.

Saving tens of thousands in your early twenties is not common, but it is possible. I learned how to adopt the frugal lifestyle while sustaining myself on a few grand in college, but I really ramped up my savings and frugal habits during the last year working. Not to mention, there were a few months where I had the income from both my job and my side hustle, which allowed me to double down. Here's how I was able to accomplish this.

Skip the Car Payment

When I was in college, I was able to drive a paid-off car thanks to my grandfather. However, this car didn't end up lasting as long as I had hoped for. After commuting back and forth to college for two years, my 2008 Chevy Cobalt was in bad shape. During my first few weeks working as a past-due bill collector, I ended up needing a different vehicle. Coincidentally, my mom was looking to upgrade her 1999 Honda CR-V at the time. Her car was in decent shape but was rusted and showing its age. I asked her if I could buy it for $2,500 and she agreed. Since I was making $27.20 an hour, I could have easily gone into a dealership and been approved for a car loan. But I didn't want to go down that route. I didn't want to saddle myself with years of car payments. Instead, I wanted to keep my expenses as low as possible. I ended up driving that car for many years before eventually selling it to my brother.

An older car does require some time and money. This is also largely dependent on what type of older vehicle you buy. Some older vehicles will be a terrible investment no matter what based on poor reliability. After driving the Honda for a while, I realized I was spending about $500 on repairs every six months. One of my friends at the utility company was a mechanic on the side, so he routinely fixed it up for me as needed. I would drive over to his house after work, and he would show me how to do things like change the oil or brake pads. Maintaining the car yourself can be a cost saver, but you have to consider the time spent doing these things as well. On the flip side, older vehicles often have a lower insurance cost. My insurance dropped by almost $100 per month when I switched vehicles. Between the insurance savings and having no car payment, I estimate that driving this beat-up old car allowed me to save close to $10,000 over the two years that I worked for the utility company. When it comes to an older car, there are other considerations, such as safety features, time spent at repair shops, and more. It may not be worth it for everyone, but it was for me. As far as what type of car you choose, skip the flashy models, and go for a reliable, fuel-efficient economy vehicle to keep your maintenance and gas costs as low as possible. The main thing to remember is to do your research beforehand on overall reliability. Every major vehicle manufacturer has had some good years and bad ones based on their different vehicle offerings.

Don't Spend Money While You're on the Clock

There was quite a bit of downtime at my job with the utility company, and it was common to hop in the truck and head over to Dunkin' Donuts for a 20-minute breakfast with my coworkers. After doing this for a few weeks, I realized that I was spending about $20 a day on breakfast and lunch, or $100 weekly. This led me to create a new frugality rule: avoid spending money while on the clock, period. The entire point of working a job, unless you are just plain bored, is to make money. It does not make sense to spend money while you are supposed to be earning it. If I spent $10 on breakfast at work, that would mean I earned $17.20 for that hour, not $27.20. After taxes, that $17 would turn into $12. Once I realized that I didn't want to stay in this job for the long haul, I immediately stopped spending money on food and drinks while I was at work. Instead, I went out and purchased a mini four-cup coffee maker, ground coffee, a tub of oatmeal, and a big jar of peanut butter. I would get to work and make my coffee and breakfast at my desk. Breakfast would consist of quick oats mixed with a little bit of peanut butter. In total, this cost me around $0.50 a day for breakfast and coffee, and there was the added health benefit of eating oats for breakfast instead of a greasy breakfast sandwich.

Lunch, on the other hand, was a bit more complicated. I realized that I would have to start prepping my meals at home, so I began doing that on Sundays for the week ahead. This also meant ordering meal prep containers, something I highly recommend doing. I settled on eating plain chicken breast, broccoli, and chickpeas for lunch. Although this is an odd combination, I've always been a fan of bland foods and I don't really grow tired of them. The total daily cost of this lunch was around $2.50. Because I often had to eat lunch in the truck while we were out on a site visit, I quickly learned to bring a cooler to avoid spending money on food. Most of my coworkers found my preference for eating a meal from home rather than going out to lunch a little antisocial, but it was important for me to stick to my rules. I followed my meal prep routine religiously for about a year before departing from that job. I would estimate that the cost savings over that year amounted to $4,500. That is a staggering amount of money spent on prepared food and coffee, especially considering that the food I prepared at home was far healthier than fast-food options.

If you are completely against prepping meals, there are a lot of companies offering healthy prepared meal deliveries. You can get your meals delivered for the week ahead, saving yourself time and money. Simply put, stop going out to breakfast or lunch at work.

Automate Your Finances

A key lesson I learned from *The Richest Man in Babylon* by George Clason is to pay yourself first. A lot of people pay everyone else before setting aside money for themselves, and there is often nothing left over at the end. Instead, this school of thought requires you to set aside money from your paycheck on payday. Back in the day, this meant physically going to a bank to cash your check and then setting some of that cash aside. Or it meant initiating a transfer with your bank. Both of these required time and energy, making it likely for people to procrastinate or not do it altogether. Today, your entire financial life can be fully automated. There are countless apps that you can use. One of my favorites is, of course, M1 Finance. (You can find my free M1 Finance training course to automate your finances at ryanoscribner.com.) With M1, you can save, invest, borrow, and spend all in one place. Apps like this give you a bird's-eye view of your entire financial life. On payday, have a certain amount of money automatically moved from your checking account over to your savings account, where you are far less likely to spend it. In order to determine this amount, sit down and get an idea of your overall income, your expenses, and the difference between them. If you don't set money aside in a savings account, you are far more likely to spend it as you see more and more money accumulating. The amount of money you divert to savings should feel a little uncomfortable for you. You need to begin challenging yourself and pushing yourself outside of your comfort zones. Don't leave yourself strapped for cash to the point that you have to use spare change to buy gas, but at the same time, putting away $25 a week isn't going to cut it either. Find something in the middle.

I accomplished this personal finance automation through a few avenues while working. First of all, I contributed a set percentage of my paycheck to my 401(k) retirement account before I even had a chance to touch it. After that, I was also directing a percentage of my post-tax income into the employee stock purchasing plan. I was able to buy shares of the power utility at a slight discount, so I took full advantage of this. Finally, I would move a few hundred into my Scottrade account to invest. At the time, I was directing all of my money toward investments. This is actually not ideal and led to a few instances of being "cash poor," having too much money in assets and not enough in cash. Make sure you have saved enough money before you begin investing.

Today, I am still a huge fan of automation. I have nearly every recurring expense on autopayment; that way there is nothing that I have to do or remember.

Minimize Housing Costs

Housing is the largest spending category for most people, so finding ways to minimize it will go a long way toward reducing your overall spending. I was able to live at home until I got my first apartment when I was 23 years old. When I started working for the utility company, I paid my mom $600 a month toward the housing expenses. This was a lot cheaper than renting my own place and having to pay for things such as internet and utilities. If I had been living out on my own, I don't think I would have been able to quit my job and grow my channel as fast as I did. Compared to most of my friends, I spent about five years longer living at home. During the two years that I was working full-time while living at home, I saved around $400 monthly. Over the course of those two years, I was able to save just shy of $10,000 in housing costs alone. Depending on your situation, you may not be able to live with family members. However, if it is at all possible, I would highly consider it. If you aren't able to live with family, look into getting one or more roommates. Splitting costs two or three ways will help tremendously.

Following these habits will enable you to spend as little money as possible, allowing you to maximize your savings. It also means that you will be able to sustain yourself for a longer period of time if you decide to transition to your side hustle full-time.

We now know that money should be viewed as a fuel source that enables you to reclaim your time. Let's cover the time frugality tips that allowed me to make the most efficient use of my reclaimed time.

Phone Calls and Meetings

If you plan on having a phone call or meeting with someone, you need to have a defined timeline and agenda for the call. While many people are just looking to pass the time, you are now trying to make the most of it. All meetings and calls need to be scheduled in advance with a given time slot.

I always tell the other person at the beginning of the call that I have a "hard stop" at a set time, which is usually whatever time the meeting was originally scheduled to end. This can work to your benefit because you are demonstrating to the other person that you either value your time a lot or are very busy. If you spend an hour and a half on an open-ended phone call with someone that branches off to discussions about pets and your social life, you're not giving the impression of being busy or in high demand.

After your call, I also recommend sending an email to that person with a bulleted summary of what was discussed on the call. This gives you a record of the call that you can reference at a later date. It's also a great time to remind the other person of any "calls to action" or next steps they have to complete on their end.

In addition, you should try to schedule all calls together in the same two- to three-hour window each day. I try to keep calls within a two-hour window from noon to 2 p.m. A lot of people will take scattered calls throughout the day, and that may be unavoidable at times. But, whenever possible, this window is a great way to cut down on interruptions throughout the day. It is better for your brain concentration and focus to complete all calls at once, so that you won't have to keep switching between different tasks. Scheduling all your calls within a set time frame also gives you the benefit of building efficiency through repetition. On days that I have multiple calls, I always set myself up with something to drink as well as a notebook to jot things down during the calls. I complete all the calls I have that day, usually with a five- to ten-minute gap between each one. Then, I send out emails with a summary of what was discussed at the end of all my calls. Whenever you can group tasks together in batches, you will be operating as efficiently as possible. You will also be cutting down on your stress by not switching back and forth between all sorts of different tasks throughout the day. I also recommend using a calendar service such as Calendly to schedule your calls.

Skip the Social Drinks

These days, it is very common to meet someone for a drink to network and build important business relationships. However, I personally don't think that alcohol should be mixed into the equation with most business meetings. If the person you are meeting with orders an alcoholic beverage, there's no reason to make them feel bad about it, but consider sticking to a nonalcoholic beverage yourself. If they make a comment about it, simply tell them you only drink on weekends. Truth be told, if you are sacrificing correctly, you shouldn't be spending any money on alcohol. This can potentially cost you hundreds of dollars weekly, depleting your fuel reserve. If I have to meet someone in person, I will usually choose a place like a cafe. I have always found conversations over a cup of tea or coffee to be far more productive than those had over a beer.

There are a few reasons for this rule. First, spending money on alcohol when you are starting a side hustle is a no-no in my book. Second, having a drink takes time, which relates to our earlier discussion on open-ended calls. Sitting down and having drinks with someone could easily turn a 30-minute conversation into a two-hour conversation. Let's be honest, most of that conversation won't be related to business. Finally, going out for drinks can derail other plans. When I started my side hustle, I knew I needed to spend every night working before bed. If I ended up going out for a beer or two, I wouldn't want to get any work done when I got home. Instead, I would end up calling it an early night and going to bed. One drink often leads to more, and it can easily eat into time you meant to spend on your side hustle.

This doesn't mean you have to abstain from drinking entirely. Networking events can be an appropriate time to have an alcoholic beverage, since you usually have the opportunity to talk to multiple people at once. I also attend a lot of conferences where brands will host parties and cocktail hours. In my opinion, this is a totally fair time to cut loose and have a drink or two.

In Lesson 1, we discussed how to rid yourself of lazy habits. One of the strategies mentioned was giving yourself a reward at the end of completing your daily tasks. I mentioned myself being motivated by a cold beer at the end of a long workday. Generally speaking, I don't see an issue with having a drink at home. Buying a six-pack at the grocery store is a lot cheaper than going out to a bar for a draft. However, it is important that this does not become a routine or habitual activity, as alcohol consumption is a slippery slope for many. You may decide to avoid alcohol altogether.

Schedule Time for Leisure

In the same way that you schedule a time slot for meetings, you should be doing the same for any leisure activities. Even while I was working full-time and side hustling at night, I did budget some time for leisure activities. I would usually wrap up work around 11 p.m. If I was tired,

I would go right to bed. If I wasn't and needed to get my mind off things, I would watch one episode of a Netflix show.

Another important consideration here is how you spend your time on weekends. I was rather dissatisfied with life in general while I was working. As a result, I decided to use my weekends to my advantage and spent most of that time working on my side hustle. I never really found much to do on the weekends that I particularly enjoyed anyway. Fast-forward to today: I have slowed down the pace a lot and value time off quite a bit. Remember, long-term consistency is the goal here. If taking Sunday afternoons off allows you to be consistent in the long run, do it. My suggestion would be to schedule that time, though, rather than keeping it open-ended. Maybe you decide to meal prep on Sunday morning, work until 3 p.m. and then take the rest of the day off.

Audit Your Time

My last piece of advice here is to self-audit your time. Most of us do not know where our time is even going. What I recommend is carrying a notebook with you for a few days and writing down everything you do. You might be surprised when you learn that you typically spend three hours a night on the couch. Jotting down your life activities for a few days is going to give you hard data to look at. Imagine if you were trying to be better at budgeting your money, but had no bank statements to look at. You would have absolutely no idea where your money was going, making this a nearly impossible task. In order to better spend your time, you need to know where this time is being spent in the first place. I recommend using a pocket notebook instead of your phone, since you are trying to cut down on screen time as well. The notebook will likely serve a dual purpose, as I also recommend keeping one with you at all times to jot down ideas.

If you have been guilty of viewing money as simply a medium of exchange, I hope this chapter exposed you to some new viewpoints surrounding money. For me, a lot changed in my life when I began viewing money as a fuel source. If I was at the mall thinking about buying a shirt, I would think about that purchase in terms of whether or not it was an effective use of my fuel. Previously, I would have just bought the shirt, using money as a means to go out and get what I want. Once I began using money to buy back my time, every dollar became minutes on the clock for me. If I spent five dollars at a coffee shop, I thought about how many minutes of my time I just gave away. "Time is money," as they say. As such, you can't be wasteful with either. Managing both effectively will give you the longest runway, or amount of time, giving you the best chance for success

Key Takeaways

- Think about money as a fuel source that needs to be conserved. Instead of spending all your money by using it as a medium of exchange, save and invest.

- Steer clear of "lifestyle inflation," which is spending more money on your wants as your income increases.

- Reduce high-cost spending categories such as your transportation and housing by driving a reliable older vehicle and living with family, if possible.

- If you are currently working at a job, avoid spending money while on the clock. Bring or make your own coffee and lunches.

- Try to schedule all your calls and meetings during the same time of day. This allows you to avoid the interruptions throughout the day.

- Leisure time is important to de-stress. However, just like with the rest of your routine, this needs to be scheduled and not open-ended.

- Spend a week tracking how you spend your time in a notebook. You will be surprised by what you find.

LESSON 6

Pick a Good Hustle

Most people choose a side hustle based on how much money they think they can make with it. As you now know, that is the wrong approach for many reasons. The biggest reason is that your side hustle should always relate back to one of your passions or natural interests. "Making money" doesn't count as a passion. I learned this lesson through the countless side hustles I tried to launch to simply make money. I would start these with a high level of intensity but would lose interest very quickly. I lacked the follow-through, or long-term consistency. If you follow your genuine interests, you are far more likely to stick it out. Maybe you loved riding horses as a kid or fixing up bicycles. Why not channel one of your childhood interests into a side hustle like I did? My passion for investing and the stock market began when I was 11. My grandmother took me on a trip to Wall Street and I was immediately hooked. Put some thought into your passions, hobbies, and childhood interests. Be sure to include past hobbies and interests as well. These will point you in the right direction.

Intensity vs. Consistency

The main factor that helped me stick with my YouTube channel was creating content about one of my longest-running interests: investing. I have always been fascinated with the stock market and investing, making this a lifelong passion of mine. I always explain this idea of intensity versus consistency as the difference between having two types of fuel propelling you forward. Think about how a rocket is launched. Typically, there are multiple engines and fuel tanks. There is a separate external tank specifically designed for the launch that detaches after the rocket has successfully launched. After that, the rocket runs off the other fuel systems within it. Short-term intensity is essentially that separate external fuel tank for a rocket launch. Sure, it can get you off the ground and maybe even a decent distance. However, it will run out quickly. Unless you have another fuel system in place, your long-term consistency, the rocket is coming back down to earth.

Let's face it: short-term intensity is exciting. It's the grind and hustle culture you see all over social media. However, that will only get you so far. It's long-term consistency over time that leads to success, which is a far more sustainable fuel source. You can still rely on short-term intensity to get your great idea started and off the ground, but don't expect to sustain yourself on that fuel source for very long. You can't get to the moon relying on the launch fuel only. You need to choose a fuel source that you can tap into with consistency.

Beyond just interests and passions, you need to make sure you are adequately prepared to launch your side hustle too. It is difficult to achieve long-term success with anything if you don't plan for it and integrate it as part of your overall routine. It's nearly impossible when you don't have a routine at all. That is why it is important to take time to develop your routine before adding a side hustle into the mix. Beyond that, it is imperative to bridge the gap between short-term intensity and long-term consistency. I tried many different business and side hustle ideas in my teenage years. I would go at each endeavor with a level of intensity that was truly not sustainable. I would end up spending all my waking hours obsessed with the project at hand. But this approach ultimately led to burnout. I wouldn't be able to keep up the pace and would stop entirely. Based on my many experiences with this, I will tell you that short-term intensity is not the goal here. Instead, you want to ask yourself what you could see yourself realistically doing each week for the next decade of your life. This reinforces the important principle of delayed gratification. Most people who are successful have simply been doing the same thing over and over for many years. Successful people rarely jump from one business to the next without careful thought and planning.

Tying my side hustle with one of my passions helped me a lot, but there is more to it than that. Blindly following your passions rarely translates to success. Instead, following a plan after laying a proper foundation does. Here's how to get a jump start on that plan.

A Business Plan

Let's talk about the process of building a house. The work involved with that starts long before the first shovel breaks ground. In order to build a house, you have to follow the necessary steps. This includes tasks like finding the land, securing funds, clearing the location, and more. To get approved for a loan by the bank, you need to have detailed plans of what you are looking to build or have built. Now, most people reading this won't be going out and getting a loan to start a side hustle. The good news is, most side hustles won't cost you much money to get started. However, you still need to have plans to work from in order to build a house or, in this case, start a side hustle.

With a side hustle, you may or may not decide to write out a formal business plan. I have only written one of these in my life and it was for a class on entrepreneurship. I hated the entire process because I found it too rigid and structured. So, it's up to you on whether or not you follow the formal outline of a business plan. The important thing here is that you have some type of plan work from. What this looks like will be different for everyone. You don't need to know exactly what you want to do yet, but you should begin writing down any thoughts you have. If you have a "light bulb moment" at any point in time, pause and go write it down.

For me, taking notes in a physical notebook works best. I tend to be the type of person who comes up with ideas all the time, often in the middle of the night. I highly recommend keeping a notebook next to your bed on a nightstand if you are one of these people as well. This can be the same notebook you use for other tasks as well, such as auditing your time.

Picking a Side Hustle

What separates a good side hustle from a bad one? When I was trying to figure out what side hustle to focus on myself, I jumped around a lot and tried many different things. I ran into common sticking points across many unrelated side hustles. Through this process, I came up with a systematic approach to find a good starting point for a side hustle. Here are the steps:

1. Write down the characteristics you're looking for in a side hustle.
2. Make a list of your passions.
3. Determine which three to four passions are most likely to make you money.
4. Determine which of those match up with your characteristics from step 1.
5. If none match, repeat the process with a larger list of passions and interests.

One day, I ended up taking a bit of an unconventional approach to figuring out my side hustle. Instead of considering specific side hustle ideas, I started by writing down the characteristics I was looking for. I came up with this: time freedom, location independence, and scalability.

By "time freedom," I meant being able to work on the side hustle at any time. Equally important, this also meant being able to *not* work on the business if I didn't want to. The number one thing I was looking for by transitioning from a job to a business was having control of my time. I hated being stuck at my desk at work, especially when I had nothing to do, which was the case most of the time. There would be times during the winter when I would have entire days go by with absolutely no work to do. I didn't want to have to occupy a desk for a set number of hours most days of the week in order to earn income. I didn't want to be held to a set work schedule, which was basically the same thing as having a job. This ruled out a lot of service-based side hustles as I would have to stick to a set schedule with clients.

Next, let's talk more about "location independence." I wanted to find a side hustle that I could work on not only around the clock, but also anywhere I was. I didn't like the idea of a side hustle or business that required you to stay in one physical location. I don't think this is such a bad idea now, but at the time I was in my early twenties looking to explore the world. Many side hustles, such as computer programming, virtual teaching, and editing services can be done anywhere—even if you are up in the Rocky

Mountains on a "work-cation." Many of my peers have taken this a step further and used the freedom of being a content creator to explore the entire world.

Finally, "scalability." I wanted to find a side hustle that would allow me to increase the earnings and revenue over time with relative ease. While my YouTube channel ended up being somewhat difficult to scale, at the time I did not think it would be. However, in the long run, I have found that online businesses in general are easy to scale. It's just a matter of being involved with the right opportunity.

This process could take you a little bit of time, but have patience. You may have to repeat the process, expanding your list of passions or compromising on some of the characteristics you are looking for. Take time to figure out what you are looking for in a side hustle before going out and finding one. This is similar to putting together criteria for your ideal partner before putting yourself out there in the dating world. If you don't know what you are looking for, how will you know when you've found it?

Side Hustle and Lifestyle Conflicts

Before going all in with an idea, you want to think about the long term. Part of this process is determining if the side hustle will conflict with what you want to do in the future. If your ultimate goal in life is to travel the world, maybe a service-based business isn't for you, since it will require you to stay in one physical place. Providing a service as a side hustle could include things like dog walking, pool skimming, or detailing cars. These may appeal to you because they require a limited amount of upfront work and capital to get started. However, these types of side hustles will require you to be in one physical location. It would be difficult to manage it from far away, especially in different time zones. Most of us are taught or instructed to schedule our lives around our job. A lifestyle business is pretty much the exact opposite; instead, you create a business around a particular type of lifestyle you are looking to live. For example, if you want to spend every day on the beach, why not teach surfing lessons? That would be a lot easier than building passive income streams that eventually allow you to sit and drink on the beach all day. Not to mention, it would be a lot more fulfilling too. Try to think about your ultimate goals or aspirations in life, and if possible, avoid starting a business that has major conflicts with your future plans.

Based on the characteristics I was looking for out of a side hustle, I was partial to an online or digital-based side hustle. These tend to be the only types of businesses out there that allow you to be location independent, give you control of your time, and are scalable. However, since this is the most desirable lifestyle, it's also the most competitive. Again, you shouldn't avoid a given side hustle just because of competition. You need to be confident that you can at the very least meet, if not exceed, the current quality bar for that niche. On the other hand, you might have no interest in online-based side hustles. Maybe your ultimate goal is to be outside and away from your computer all day.

On days where I spend 12 hours staring at a computer screen, I often think about offline businesses. There is a lot of value in human interaction, something you tend to miss out on with digital-based businesses today.

My Side Hustle Recommendations

So, back to side hustles: What is the best one to get started with right now? Well, that answer is going to be different depending on what you are good at, the characteristics you are looking for, and your passions. I am going to share a few side hustles that stand out to me now or have worked well for me and others. Not all side hustles out there are created equally. There are some that are easy to scale with high profit margins. And others can be a frustrating experience for almost all who participate. For example, starting a restaurant would be a difficult side hustle for many reasons. Instead, here are some great places to start.

1. NICHE BLOGGING

If you are more introverted but naturally curious about different topics, such as fly fishing, saving money through couponing, or creating travel guides, this could be the perfect side hustle for you. For this side hustle, you need to determine something about which you are both curious and knowledgeable that you would be interested in writing about. Of course, competition should be considered as well. If you decide on a few topics, look at what is out there and evaluate the competition. Figure out where the quality bar currently stands.

Not everyone is going to want to quit their job and do their side hustle full-time, and that is totally fine. For those people, a niche blog could be the perfect fit based on the minimal amount of maintenance and time commitment. In addition, the costs associated with starting a blog are extremely low. You basically need a laptop, internet access, a domain name, and a hosting plan. If you already have a laptop and internet access, the rest of that is going to run you about $100 for your first year. There aren't a lot of side hustles you can start with a $100 bill, but blogging is definitely one of them. What you will learn, however, is that blogging takes a while to get off the ground. In fact, it's not uncommon at all to see almost no traffic for the first six months. You have to consider that there are billions of websites out there, and Google indexes most of them. When you first start blogging, Google is pretty much going to ignore you. You won't find your site showing up in search results anywhere. But, if you keep at it, you will see articles rank and begin bringing in traffic over time.

I'm currently involved with operating the following blogs/sites:

- **InvestingSimple.com:** Personal finance and investing app review and comparison site. Content is written in a simple manner; no finance degree is required to understand what you are reading.

- **ryanoscribner.com:** This is where I link out to my free trainings and different "bridge pages." Recently, I've been adding original content to this site as well.
- **FarmlandRiches.com:** This blog is related to the ins and outs of investing in farmland, something I am passionate about preserving having grown up in "redneck" farm country.
- **RowingBasics.com:** Rowing on a home machine is one of my favorite ways to get a quick workout in. My latest blog is all about home rowing machines and the benefits this type of exercise can provide.

Keep in mind that even though I have many sites, I built them up one at a time. I launched my personal brand website in 2016, followed by Investing Simple in 2018 and Farmland Riches in 2021. I currently have a portfolio of dozens of domains and plans to launch a new blog every year or two, with Rowing Basics being my latest blog project.

2. YOUTUBE CHANNEL

A YouTube channel is another solid option if you are looking to do a side hustle alongside your current job. You certainly can scale a channel up like I did and go full-time, but I also know many part-time YouTubers who make a few thousand dollars each month in addition to the income from their job. It can be a pretty awesome gig. In the past, I've recommended the path of blogging to people who are more introverted and YouTube to those who are more extroverted. However, I was more introverted before starting my channel, and it really helped me come out of my shell. Don't rule out the idea of a YouTube channel just because you don't want to be on camera. We recently started testing AI-generated content for the Investing Simple YouTube channel. Through the use of cloud-based software, we're able to turn our best articles into quick YouTube videos by leveraging artificial intelligence. So far, we are seeing great results, with some of these videos getting over 1,000 views in the first few months.

It's important to think about what types of YouTube channels have success today. For starters, let's cover some topics that are less likely to succeed. Vlogging about your life, personality channels, and travel channels are on that list. Most people are just entirely too busy to watch vlogs today. Unless you have a really, really interesting life, such as being a professional alligator wrestler, or you happen to be a billionaire, people will not care about what you are doing day to day. The same is true of personality channels, or a channel just about yourself. While you can weave in personal elements to your channel, which can help build a better connection with your audience, you should not be the central topic of your channel.

Finally, travel and comedy content are so competitive at this point that I don't think it's worth going into. Unless you already have tens of thousands of dollars' worth of equipment, film and editing know-how, as well as the means to travel all over the world, skip this one. As for the comedy channels, you will need to tie your humor in with something else in order for people to find your content.

For example, maybe it's a funny spin on the daily news. Simply being funny is not enough today.

I'm currently involved with operating the following channels:

- Ryan Scribner YouTube channel
- Investing Simple YouTube channel
- Farmland Riches YouTube channel

3. GIG WORKER

If you have a digital skill that is in demand, one of the easiest ways to get started with a side hustle is offering remote services through online gig work. The gig economy has truly exploded over the last few years. Businesses like mine often do not have full-time employees, but instead have a lot of independent contractors—individuals who perform a service for someone else as a freelancer. With my channel and blogs alone, we have close to two dozen different gig workers helping us out. The gig work ranges from writing services to social media, graphic design, and more. Typically, independent contractors are paid by the hour or by the project. As an independent contractor, you have the ability to control your schedule. Since you aren't an employee, you aren't held to nearly the same strict standards. You work when you want, check your email when you want, and have a lot of control over your life.

The best way to get started with gig work is to post ads for your services on websites like Fiverr and Upwork.

These sites harness the skills of freelancers all over the world, making it easy for people to hire gig workers on a per-hour basis. While it's free to post on these sites, they do take a cut of your sales. You can use sites like these to launch your side hustle, leveraging the skills of millions of freelancers by hiring them for your gigs. For example, if you plan on being a freelance graphic designer, you could hire someone on Fiverr to help you create a website in order to market your services. You could then post your own gig on Fiverr as a means for additional exposure. The possibilities here are truly endless.

Let's touch on your website a bit more, as this is a tremendously important asset for your soon-to-be side hustle. When creating your own website, I'm partial to a self-hosted WordPress website. However, you can explore "site builder" options. An example is Beacons.ai, one of the many start-ups I've invested in. This tool is the easiest way to create a "link in bio" website for free. You might have to start off cheap with your services just to get the ball rolling, but once you have reviews coming in, you can bump up your prices. Eventually, the goal would be to ditch those gig work websites entirely and cut out the middleman, working directly with clients. This is also a business you could scale as well. If you are doing graphic design, for example, you could eventually hire people to do that design work for you while you focus on other aspects of the business.

4. AIRBNB TOUR GUIDE

Here's one you may not have considered. Have you lived in the same area for many years? If so, you are probably an unofficial expert on that area. Sites like Airbnb have made it extremely easy to offer experiences to tourists visiting your area. While they may take a cut of your earnings, they are supplying you with a never-ending stream of tourists looking for things to do in your area. Visitors are able to book experiences on Airbnb after they book a stay, and you could offer one of those experiences. While you could go big and do something like Jet Ski rentals, why not start small?

I remember a trip to Seattle where I ended up booking a pub crawl with a local tour guide as an experience. The pub crawl ended up including myself and another couple. The experience itself was $50, and we had to cover the cost of our beers at the different bars. It was a really fun time, and we ended up tipping him another $20 each at the end. In total, this tour guide made $210 for roughly three hours of work. Not to mention, what is required for this business outside of some basic knowledge and an app on your phone? Even if you aren't an expert on your local area, you could easily brush up on your information and become one. There are tons of other experiences you could offer on Airbnb, so consider this and get creative!

5. EXPERIENCE-BASED BUSINESS

If you think back to JCPenney and the Golden Rule, so many people visited these stores over and over again because of the positive experience they had there. While it's unlikely that anyone will be starting a department store as their side hustle, there are lessons to be learned here.

You should have the goal of creating an experience for your customer. For example, if you're an expert on Italian food, you could do paid virtual cooking classes on how to make pasta with feedback given in real time. Or, if you know a lot about wine, create a video on wine tasting, becoming an affiliate for the wine mentioned in the video. These are just two examples of experience-based side hustles that provide value to others while still falling under your own personal area of interest. If you don't know enough about a specific subject to create an experience for others, study hard and learn about one you are interested in! I scoured bookstores for books on personal development and investing, which eventually made me a self-taught expert on both.

Experience, or "wow factor," can be applied to most product-based businesses out there. Creating a personal experience separates you from others, and it's often difficult for large companies to personalize at scale. For example, let's say you have a side hustle selling bath bombs. You could create a website form that asks people for their favorite color, scent, and gemstone. Using that information, you could make their bath bomb a completely personalized experience. It's easy for you to do this, but it would be difficult for a large e-commerce company to do this. This is one of the only advantage side hustlers have over large businesses, so use this advantage to its fullest!

The good news is, you can sell an experience or something personalized both online and in a traditional brick-and-mortar business. It doesn't take much to go from selling a product to an experience. What it comes down to is putting yourself in the shoes of your customer and going back to the Golden Rule. How would you want to be treated, and what would make this the most special experience for you?

6. "REAL WORLD" SIDE HUSTLE

While online-based side hustles are certainly glamorous, there is a lot to love about "real world" side hustles too. What I am referring to is any side hustle that brings you out of your house and into the real world. For example, when my fiancée and I moved to Miami Beach, we decided to test one of these "real world" side hustles. After watching a great series called *Undercover Billionaire*, we were inspired to try out our own business. After brainstorming ideas, we decided on a juice business. Following the strategy of bootstrapping, or spending as little as possible to get the business started, we went to Goodwill and purchased a used cooler and juicer. We then picked up some jars and local produce. After a thorough cleaning, we put the cooler outside with a few jars of juice sitting on ice. We ended up selling a few jars each day for $5 each and documenting the process for a video series.

Based on the appealing characteristics mentioned earlier, most people are interested in an online-based side hustle. This makes them highly competitive. There are far fewer out there who are looking to start something in the real world. This gives you an advantage over others, seeing as you are willing to put in the hard work. I personally view this as an area that is overlooked by many.

A Side Hustle Pitfall

When researching side hustles and business ideas online, beware of people who may be looking to separate you from your money. One example of this can be paid educational programs, be it in person or online. (To be clear, this is outside of a college setting.) I'm not here to say that all online courses or programs are a waste of money. I've spent thousands of dollars on them, many of which I would consider a great investment. Some, on the other hand, were a complete waste of time and money. Instead, I would encourage you to explore free online content first. What someone is selling with an online course is the convenience of having all of that information in one place. If the price they are asking is worth the convenience, by all means go for it. The side hustle pitfall to avoid is paying for information that you could get elsewhere for free. That is simply because you would be spending money you don't need to spend, wasting one of your most important resources. If the paid information is able to get you where you need to go faster, saving you time, it could be worthwhile.

All of us had childhood interests and dreams. Even if we have lost touch with them as adults, it is important to revisit them as these will help guide you to your ideal side hustle. If you follow the ideas in this chapter, you can uncover some of the best opportunities out there today. Even if you are not an expert on a specific topic, you can become one by simply learning. Just like I did, you can pick up books or utilize free online resources to become an expert over time. Keep in mind as well that the best side hustle tomorrow probably doesn't exist yet. When I was a kid, there was no such thing as being a content creator as a side hustle. Pay attention to trends and stay on the cutting edge of things. For example, what might be some future NFT, blockchain, or metaverse-related side hustles?

Key Takeaways

- The key to long-term success with a side hustle is finding out how to make money through one of your passions.

- Create a written plan to follow. This doesn't have to be a formal business plan, but it does have to be in writing, not just in your head.

- Short-term intensity is not the goal. Instead, ask yourself what you could realistically see yourself doing every week for the next decade of your life.

- Digital skills are in high demand. If you don't have one now, you can learn one using free online resources. One of the easiest side hustles to start is gig work through sites like Upwork and Fiverr.

- While competition is an important consideration, don't avoid a niche just because it is competitive.

As long as you can meet or exceed the quality bar, you have a chance of breaking through.

- There are tons of sites and apps that make it easy to launch a side hustle, including Airbnb. Offering tours of your local area as an Airbnb experience is an easy way to start bringing in some extra money on the side.

Find a Mentor

We all come into our side hustle journey with a set of beliefs about ourselves. While some of these beliefs may be positive, a lot of them are negative. These negative beliefs about yourself may no longer serve you well in life. Despite this, they are often difficult to overcome. Such beliefs are known as *limiting beliefs*, preconceived notions about yourself that prevent you from reaching your goals and becoming the best version of yourself.

Limiting beliefs are often formed either by someone else's perception of you or by your own negative experiences. Usually, they are deeply rooted in past childhood experiences. An example of a childhood incident causing a limiting belief could be if you had a teacher say that math wasn't for you. You might internalize their opinion without even knowing it. This might lead you to avoid math-related tasks or jobs in the future. Ironically, you might've been good at math had you pursued it. Similarly, if you had some negative experiences in high school gym class, you might believe that sports aren't for you. While there are some cases where you can overcome these limiting beliefs on your own, a helping hand from someone you trust can speed along the process.

Educating myself by reading and exploring online resources helped me overcome a lot of my limiting beliefs about money. I also made guided meditations part of my daily routine, many of which were focused on limiting beliefs. However, I wasn't able to overcome all of my limiting beliefs on my own. Before quitting my job, I doubted that I would be able to succeed with my YouTube channel. I was only able to get past some of these deeply rooted limiting beliefs about myself with the help of my mentor.

What Is a Mentorship?

A mentorship can mean many different things. In most cases, it's when someone offers you guidance because their prior experience matches your future goals. Mentorships can come in two forms: personal or professional. Professional mentorships often support you with your professional goals; this can also include overcoming any business or financial-related limiting beliefs, in addition to sharing business skills with you. On the other hand, a personal mentorship tackles deeper-rooted limiting beliefs. A personal mentor could help you boost your self-worth by showing you how to reframe the way you look at your past. The main thing all mentors have in common is showing you, the mentee, that all the power to do things is already within you. They are just helping you realize that. Most of the negative thoughts about yourself, if not all of them, can and should be let go. Through this process, you are ensuring that there is nothing in your way or holding you back mentally.

There's usually a clear distinction between being mentored about personal and professional limiting beliefs. But, like me, you may need a mix of both. My first mentor knew me on a personal level for several years prior to becoming my mentor. Based on his own success and self-education, he had a lot to teach me about business. If you have a family member or close friend who has a business or knowledge of business skills, they could teach you valuable lessons, such as making short- and long-term plans, managing cash flow, or even bookkeeping. For example, my uncle, an accountant, gave me spreadsheet lessons many years ago when I first started making money and needed to keep track of it. As these people are already close to you, they can help you with some of your more personal limiting beliefs, maybe even in addition to teaching you about business.

My Mentor Experience

My first mentor was Jake Woodard, a close friend from college and a colleague at the utility company. It's funny how things came to be. It was very informal; I didn't even know that I was looking for a mentor. I was working in the design department then and had been in a rut for a few months. I felt stagnant. I had entirely too much time on my hands at the desk job in the design department, and I had also picked up a few bad habits that were totally out of character for me. I was eating crappy food, sleeping my weekends away, not exercising, and smoking a few cigarettes a day. On my lunch breaks, I would get fast food, eat quickly, and then sit in my car smoking a cigarette and blasting angry music. It was a very unhealthy routine, but I was stuck repeating this cycle again and again. It was as if my life was on autopilot, or as if I was in the movie *Groundhog Day*. I felt like I was living the same day over and over. After a few months of this, I realized I was digging myself further and further into a hole through this repetition. I knew I needed help, so I called Jake for some life advice. He was in incredible shape, and always seemed to be in a positive mood regardless of the challenges he was facing.

I decided to have Jake help me get back on track physically. After switching from past-due bill collections to my permanent position, I had put on some weight, and I wanted to work it off. This started with a brutal Sunday workout session. Afterward, sitting outside at the picnic table, Jake asked me if I was happy at my design job. I had to be honest with him and tell him no. Sure, the money was good, but that was about it. When I told him this, he smiled at me and told me that he knew how I felt.

Like me, Jake took a menial entry-level job with the idea of bidding into a better one. Jake wanted to get into the overhead line department, but his time spent as a meter reader helped him realize that wasn't the path he wanted to be on. He told me that he planned on quitting the job in the near future, and that he was simply preparing himself now. Jake's job as a meter reader meant that he had to drive a vehicle around for six to seven hours a day, following a red line on a screen. He told me that it was the most mind-numbing and boring job, but he figured out how to make the most of it. Like me, he was doing the same thing week in and week out, feeling trapped in life. He decided to mix things up by listening to audiobooks and podcasts. Turning his vehicle into a "mobile class-room," as he called it, helped him feel better. He encour-aged me to do the same in order to make the most of my commute, and to cut down on the angry music.

Jake then asked me what I wanted to do with my life. I had no response because I had no life goals at the time. I had thought that I wanted to be a union utility worker. I had even spent two years in college preparing for this goal. Not to mention, my grandfather had invested $10,000 into my college education, so I felt like I owed it to him to see this through. But I was feeling emotionally drained at this job, and I wasn't doing anything about it. Since Jake could tell that I had no long-term goals and a fair amount of time on my hands, he helped me find a direction to go in. We sat down and talked for over an hour. He helped me create a diet and exercise routine and said that I needed to go out and buy a copy of *Rich Dad, Poor Dad* immediately. I had nothing to lose, so I followed what Jake said to the smallest detail. I literally left the gym and went to The Fresh Market for the food, followed by Barnes & Noble for the book. I wanted to be like him. That night, I did a complete overhaul of my diet and tossed out all my junk food, based on exactly what Jake had mapped out for me. I also began following his rigorous six-day-a-week exercise regimen.

I followed this exercise and eating regimen perfectly, no cheat days or skipped workouts. A few weeks after this meeting with Jake, I decided to take things a step further. I was feeling better than I had in years, and I wanted to keep up the pace. I decided that I would not only follow what Jake told me to do, but I would also begin emulating his actions. I studied how Jake prepared for his eventual escape. I knew that I wanted to get out of this job, but I had no clue how I would do that. By watching Jake navigate that challenge himself, I realized I could learn and plan for my own escape. As such, I began studying what Jake was doing very closely.

One of the first things I noticed about Jake was his use of social media. He was posting short videos on Facebook talking about nutrition, fitness, and other wellness-related topics. In addition, he would livestream to his social media platforms each night and answer questions. A few weeks later, I would find myself doing something similar. I began creating short video content for others, but instead of Facebook, I posted on YouTube. I also followed his driving classroom idea. Each morning, I would drive to work listening to an episode of *School of Greatness*, a podcast showcasing entrepreneur success stories. Instead of blasting angry music, I was reprogramming my mind for success. Hearing about success over and over again helped me believe that it was possible for me as well. Through shedding a lot of my limiting beliefs, I realized you have to be careful about your overall consumption of positive versus negative media. Repeating angry songs over and over could make you an unhappy individual, since your brain internalizes all of this. Switching gears to a positive type of content like motivational podcasts meant I was repeating messages about success over and over again instead. Within a few weeks, I felt like I had reprogrammed my brain. People around me started commenting about how cheerful and positive I was all of a sudden.

Jake and I met again a few months after. At this point, I was in incredible physical shape and had started to expand my vision. We met for coffee, and Jake told me he would be leaving his job in January and moving to Dallas, Texas. That was only a few short months away. I was shocked that, for the first time, he had a clear timeline. I had a hard time not getting emotional when I heard this. Jake had been my light at the end of the tunnel for months, and I was going to lose him soon. I wasn't sure if I was ready to navigate things on my own, but it was clear that the time had come. He stuck to his word and ended up quitting even sooner than expected. I was envious that he had the courage to leave a "cushy" job. He then, once again, turned things over to me and asked what my plan was to get out. I didn't quite have one yet, but the gears were turning. Jake held my feet to the flames and told me to come up with something, so I decided to explore the idea of YouTube.

Jake had encouraged me to turn my vehicle into a mobile classroom, which I did during my commutes, but I spent many hours a day idle at my cubicle. I decided to deploy this strategy at my desk as well, quietly listening to podcasts and YouTube videos. If someone talked to me, I learned the hotkey command to mute my sound, so I could hear them and respond immediately. One day, I searched for the stock market on YouTube, and that's when I found the video from Jack Chapple I mentioned earlier. This video he did on the stock market, which amassed millions of views, sparked the idea. After doing further research into the niche, I came across another channel called Financial Education, which had tons of views too. I realized I had unearthed an opportunity. From that point on, I hunkered down for two months working on content. I didn't do anything except for work, exercise, and focus on this project.

Jake and I had coffee once more before he left for Dallas, and I told him about my big idea. Jake thought it was a fantastic idea. I mentioned that I had about 50 videos recorded, mostly off the cuff. He asked me why I hadn't posted any videos yet, and I told him that I was still trying to overcome my fear of putting myself out there. After talking with him about this at length, I realized this fear largely stemmed from concerns about credibility. I was a 21-year-old kid with a degree in electrical construction; who would listen to me? During the nine months that I was working on my side hustle before going full-time, Jake helped me overcome a lot of my limiting beliefs. He helped me realize I was credible in these subjects, and I soon posted my videos all at once. Although it was far from an overnight success, jumping into the deep end without a safety net was a very important step. Rather than dipping my toes in the water, I decided to go all in by posting everything at once.

Jake helped me tremendously in terms of getting on the right course in life. He followed his plan and quit his job at the end of the year, just like he said he would. In fact, he quit even earlier after learning that they would simply cut him a check for his unused vacation time. After that, he packed up his car and hit the road. After Jake moved to Dallas, we stayed in touch and I had shared that I was making about $1,000 monthly from my channel, and that I had 10,000 subscribers. After hearing that, Jake was convinced I was ready to make my escape. But I resisted. I stayed in my cubicle because I didn't fully believe in myself. One Monday afternoon, he sent me a photo of himself sitting by the pool with his laptop. I was extremely jealous, but also annoyed. I felt like he was taunting me with something that I couldn't achieve. I replied with a long text explaining that "just because you quit your job doesn't mean that I have to." In response to that text, he encouraged me to take a page out of the Nike playbook and "Just do it." So, believe it or not, I did. Ten minutes after 4 p.m., I walked out for good. I left my badge on my desk, texted my supervisor from the parking lot, and that was it.

Part of the reason Jake was so persistent was because he knew that something more than money was holding me back. I did not believe in myself, and I would have stayed at that job for months longer, if not a year, if Jake hadn't lit a fire under my butt. He knew exactly what to do and say to motivate me. I didn't realize it at the time, but Jake was helping me overcome one of my biggest limiting beliefs about myself: Am I enough? Keep in mind, though, I was well prepared. Jake knew I had adopted minimal expenses, had proven the concept with my channel, and had a significant amount in savings after living at home. There was still risk involved, but it was manageable.

What a Mentor Isn't

Jake was a huge influence and inspiration during the time that I started my side hustle, and he continues to be today. However, this is not always the case with a mentor relationship. That is because not all mentors or coaches are in this line of work for the right reasons. Some make a lot of money by manipulating their clients. I have met many people who have spent thousands of dollars on mentorship workshops or coaching programs with little to show for it. It's possible that some of these people have gone on to have success that I am unaware of, but at the time that I met them, they were all stuck in the phase of analysis paralysis. This is when you are so caught up in the idea of a business that you end up doing nothing.

As you search for a mentor, remember to look out for people trying to take advantage of you. There are people out there selling "solutions" that most of us do not need in order to start or grow a business. I met someone like this shortly after I went full-time on YouTube. He took down my number at a mixer and soon reached out asking if he could buy me coffee sometime. I agreed, but within five minutes of meeting with him, I knew that he wasn't offering anything of value. He began telling me about his business coaching, and how he could really help me grow my business if I kept him on retainer for $2,000 a month. It was an immediate no, of course, but the sales pitch didn't end there. He pressured me to fill out a painful business audit worksheet that wasn't even applicable to my online business. It was an uncomfortable situation for me as a 21-year-old, because he was the age of my father and I had always been taught to respect and look up to adults. It was challenging to say no to someone much older than me. As you begin to look for mentors, be aware of this kind of predatory behavior, and be prepared to have uncomfortable conversations.

The consulting and coaching industry is worth billions of dollars for a reason. People need help, and they will always be looking for help, whether for personal reasons or professional. However, a mentor is not a consultant or a life coach. A mentor should be someone who shares big picture ideas with you and allows you to independently apply and modify those ideas. A mentor should be someone who prioritizes helping you over making money off you. If you are in need of a life coach, someone who shows you how to complete day-to-day tasks, this should be completely separate from a mentorship.

How to Evaluate a Mentor

To me, a mentor is someone who guides you based on their experience. As such, one of the very first things you should consider is whether or not your mentor has the experience you are looking for. Jake had the exact experience I was looking for, so he was able to guide me based on sharing what worked for him in the past. It might be helpful to ask yourself these questions when vetting a potential mentor.

How do I know this person? It's important to consider if you already know a potential mentor or if they are someone who has just recently popped into your life. Right off the bat, this was a bad sign for coffee shop guy. I had only met him once, at a business networking event. Jake was able to help me because he knew me for five years before becoming my mentor. In addition, I approached him about the relationship, not the other way around. Because of our history, he knew me well and was able to identify the areas where I needed the most guidance.

Where is this person at in life, and is that where I want to be? You should never be in a mentorship in which your mentor is somewhere that you don't want to be. If you want to be a successful business owner, your mentor should not be someone who is living paycheck to paycheck. If your mentor is someone with whom you have an existing relationship, you will already have a good idea of where they are on their journey. It should be easy for you to discern whether or not they are where you want to be. If they are very private and share little details about their wealth or success, this is a red flag.

What am I providing to them in return? There are many ways to provide value to someone in exchange for mentorship. On occasion, I paid Jake a few hundred dollars for putting together meal plans or diet plans for me. He never formally charged me; I just felt like it was the right thing to do. Today, we simply exchange information and help each other out with different business-related challenges. Another great option outside of directly paying someone for their time is offering to work for them for free. This is the apprenticeship model of a mentorship, in which you learn by working for someone. I was able to provide this experience to a college student, Andrew "Apple" Crider. He sent me an email offering to work for me for free. I told him that he had a deal. After the first few days, I offered to pay him $100 weekly because I was really impressed with what he was doing. This gave him the opportunity to learn from me and eventually emulate many of my strategies to build his own personal brand.

How to Find a Mentor

These days, it can be more challenging to meet people in the real world than it used to be. Through my time spent in various customer service roles, I've become more of an extrovert. However, I wasn't always like that. I spent months getting over my shyness by following social exercises that I would give myself. For example, on my lunch break at work, I would make myself go to Walmart and ask five people what time it was. This may seem like a simple task, but if you are as introverted as I was, the idea of this probably sends chills down your spine. Think back to our lesson on skill improvement, and look at socializing as a skill you may need to improve on. Being able to comfortably communicate with others and seek out social situations gives you the benefit of growing your roster of connections. In order to have true wealth, you need to be rich both in people and in money. A lot of people solely focus on monetary wealth and miss out on the value relationships with people can bring you. In addition, you should be ready to offer those who help you a favor in return later on. You should always operate from the standpoint of providing value to others, which puts you in a position to receive value in return, be it in the form of money, relationships, or information.

Here are some suggestions on finding mentors or making connections.

Think about the qualities you're looking for in a mentor. This may sound weird, but I like to think of it like figuring out your ideal romantic partner. Write these qualities down in your notebook. Are you looking for someone to bounce ideas off? Or someone with a positive personality to motivate you? Or someone who's already knowledgeable about your business who can answer specific questions? This will help you know whether or not your first meetup with a mentor is the right fit. In addition, this might give you clues as to where you might physically find this person in the world. For me, what I needed mostly was tough love. Jake was able to provide me with exactly that, being hard on me at times and pushing me when I needed it.

Interact with the world. In the same way your perfect partner was or is out there in the world today, so is your ideal mentor. During times that I found myself socially deprived, my mom reminded me of something her friend told her: you won't meet someone new in your living room. Going out to a coffee shop or cocktail bar is a great way to meet people. (However, that comes with the important caveat that you are not overspending. Networking, which could include social drinks or food, needs to be budgeted.) Not only can you work on your social skills, but you might also end up meeting someone who could help you with your specific needs.

Join a group focused on your area of business. LinkedIn is a great place to find leads. Or check apps such as Meetup that host business functions, most of which are free. Then, make acquaintances. No, you can't simply walk around a room asking for mentors. They need to come organically. Instead, talk with people and get to know some business friends over time.

Ask people what they do and how they feel about it—and listen to what they say. This is especially helpful if you aren't quite sure what you want to do as a side hustle yet. You could find someone who's happy with their work who can be a positive force for you. In addition, this could give you some excellent clues and ideas into your future side hustle.

Find something that works for you to continue the conversation. Just like with dating, the transition point is difficult. In sales, it's called closing. For any type of relationship to prosper, you need to keep communication going. Keep in mind that a lot of high-up individuals have "gatekeepers," staff members who monitor their email and social media profiles. They might be willing to give you their number in person but be completely unreachable otherwise. Beyond asking for a number, another step could be to ask them if you can buy them a cup of coffee or meet them for breakfast. Use phrases like "I'm looking to learn more and would love to pick your brain" to make it clear what you're seeking. Otherwise, the person might think you're asking them for a job interview.

Follow up. Keep an organized list of new people you've met and how your conversation ended. Many people need a couple of invitations for coffee before they respond. Remember, they are busy professionals and don't want to be annoyed or chased. Keep it low-key. You could also use the strategy of jotting down notes about the person or interaction after it happens. These conversational anecdotes can come in handy.

Success in business comes from laying a proper foundation. Part of that means making sure you have nothing holding you back mentally. I had a lot of doubts about myself early on, especially related to credibility. Jake taught me how to overcome my limiting beliefs through self-education. He put me on the correct track, and I decided to stay on it because I liked the way it felt, both physically and emotionally. I trusted him to lead me somewhere better than I currently was. As both my professional and personal mentor, Jake was able to figure out how to motivate me. It didn't take him long to figure out that the best way to do this was to challenge me. A mentorship can help unlock the potential your mentor sees in you. Jake saw potential in me that I did not see in myself. Years later, I have switched roles and mentored a few people. Jake Woodard has also changed gears, focusing on spiritual healing guidance instead of business mentorships. By helping others in the same way Jake helped me, I like to think that I'm passing the torch. I encourage you to do the same as you continue your side hustle journey, as this is one of the most rewarding experiences you will have.

Key Takeaways

- Limiting beliefs are preconceived notions we have about ourselves. Usually, they come from past experiences. These belief systems hold us back from reaching our full potential.

- A mentor is simply someone who guides you based on their past experiences. You should always make sure that your mentor is someone you look up to.

- Watch out for mentors or coaches who are simply trying to make money. Vet a potential mentor before committing to any type of program with them.

- Instead of paying someone, offer to work for them for free. This way, they can teach you how to do things through an apprenticeship.

- Offer to buy a potential mentor coffee or lunch. These short conversations are often the most valuable in the long run.

- In order to have success in the long run, you need to be both people-rich and money-rich.

- Socializing is a skill. It should be practiced often and mastered.

Make Your First $100

When I first started exploring side hustle ideas, it was from my desk at work, in between tasks while trying to look busy. I wanted to figure out how to make enough to replace the income from my job, since I was unhappy. I didn't want to spend my life in a cubicle. I read article after article online about people who made tens of thousands of dollars a month or more doing all sorts of different things. One person I read about was Pat Flynn and his website Smart Passive Income. On this site, he shared income reports that showed earnings of over $100,000 monthly. I was so envious that I convinced myself it was fake. I wanted to be like him and others but had no idea how to start making a lot of money, or even enough to replace the income from my job. I wanted freedom like my mentor but had no clue what to do. After stressing out over this for a week or so, I came to a funny realization. Here I was trying to figure out how to make thousands of dollars per month when I hadn't even made $100 yet. Not even $100 per month—I'm talking about just $100. Earning your first $100 through a side hustle is like learning how to ride a bicycle. You will undoubtedly have some moments where you fall and scrape your knee, especially after you take off the training wheels. The important thing is to keep getting back up. You need to focus on this initial milestone before moving on to larger financial goals. In the same way you needed training wheels for your bicycle, you need to complete this side hustle challenge of making your first $100 before moving on to $100 per month and beyond.

Lessons from Running

I learned these lessons about starting small and incremental improvement while working out. This was long before my time with Jake Woodard. Here's the situation: I would frequently get picked on about my weight in college. While I caught some flak in high school, people were generally pretty tame. College was an entirely different experience. I was being harassed in the parking lot. I had also gone through a recent breakup, so I decided to channel all those sad feelings into self-improvement. My desire to escape the bullying plus the breakup provided me with a great short-term "launch fuel" source to get my fitness regimen off the ground. The day I started exercising, I went upstairs to the track at the YMCA. I figured that jogging a mile would be a good benchmark to track my progress. After running a mile for the first time in around three years, my lungs were on fire. My time was just over 12 minutes. Still, it was a start, and I was proud of myself.

Over the next few months, I would rinse and repeat. Once I got used to the running, I started adding free weights into the mix. I was doing weight training and finishing up with a mile five or six days a week. By the time spring came around, I realized I was able to run a 5K. My speed had improved tremendously too. I was challenging myself on both distance and speed. Since the weather was nice, I started running a 5K outside every day. I got to the point where I was able to run a 5K in around 20 minutes. A few months later, I decided to test myself and run the longest distance I could for a benchmark. I ended up running just over nine miles.

It took me about a year, but commitment to training had resulted in remarkable improvement. I went from barely being able to run an out-of-breath mile to being able to continuously run nine miles. I tested my mile speed at the end of the summer and my time was 6:18. I had just about cut my time by half. These were both huge accomplishments for me, considering that fitness was never a focus in my life prior to this. Starting by running one mile was a first step in the right direction. From that point forward, long-term consistency took over and did the rest of the work for me. I just had to show up.

Running a Marathon vs. Running a Mile

So how does running relate to business? It's all about completing milestones through incremental progress. If I asked you to come up with a business idea that profits $5,000 a month, you would probably be a bit overwhelmed by that task, just like I was sitting at my desk years ago reading passive income reports online. However, if I instead asked you for a plan to make $100 in the next month, could you come up with an idea? Making a plan for $100 is far more realistic and attainable for most people. As a result, more people would be willing to try it. Since it's relatively easy to accomplish, most who try will have success. This will, in turn, lead to future wins as they tend to build upon each other. You may have long-term goals of making thousands or even millions every single month. That is fantastic, and I encourage you to maintain those long-term goals. However, for now, I want you to think of a short-term goal: making your first $100 from a side hustle.

The question becomes, how can you start making your first $100 outside of a job? The answer is that you will need to provide value to someone. This could be in the form of a product you sell or a service you offer or provide. There is a specific strategy in business that most follow when it comes to determining how you will be providing this value. While the product or service will vary based on what side hustle you choose, there is an easy process to follow that applies to any niche: the Minimum Viable

Product (MVP). The MVP is something that allows you to gain maximum market insight with minimal effort. It is your way to see if your idea is good or not without going all in. It's also going to be your ticket for making your first $100 from a side hustle and completing a key milestone. This MVP strategy focuses on testing the market with a simple version of the product or service you plan on providing. The MVP strategy is often applied to the tech field, where entrepreneurs build landing pages for their product or service and test interest based on responses to social media ads. Think about that for a moment. With the tools available today, you are able to get near-instant feedback with a small investment in ads by testing conversion on landing pages for product or service ideas. In simple terms, this means creating a page with some photos and text about what you plan on launching, including an email opt-in to join the wait list. You would then spend money on ads, usually around $1,000 or so, and see what percentage of people "converted," or signed up for your email wait list, versus the number that solely clicked.

The MVP approach will also help you narrow your focus. Instead of thinking of every possible thing your idea could do, pick one. That one thing you pick should be the easiest and fastest to test. I constantly come across people who are stuck in the idea phase, generating idea after idea and never following through. One person I met told me he had over 375 different business ideas written down in the notes section of his phone. In my experience, success comes from getting good at something new and then repeating a lot of the same boring things over and over.

Sure, every few months or so there may be a strategy shift. However, most of the time it is a consistent process of rinsing and repeating.

Following the MVP Approach

Let's consider what the MVP approach might look like in action. Say you want to create a dating app. If tasked with this project, many people would start out by making a long list of features and ideas. If the ideas on this list were put into reality, all those fancy features would need to be rolled out through a series of updates over time, which would be a costly endeavor, as app developers are in high demand today. Here's the problem: if your dating app isn't the next big thing, all the different updates and versions you've planned, or even potentially started working on, are for nothing. Even if your app gets some traction, the dating space is extremely competitive. It took me a while to learn this, but not all good ideas translate to a profitable business. A lot of dating apps out there are willing to lose money in order to acquire customers, making this one of the most competitive categories out there. You could have potentially wasted months of time and money mapping out an idea that eventually goes nowhere. This waste of energy and resources is more common than you would expect, especially in the app and technology space.

What if you followed the MVP approach to this dating app idea instead? In that scenario, you would figure out how to create the most basic representation of what you felt was the key noteworthy feature of your app. If it was

Tinder, maybe this is the all-important swipe feature. You could then create a short survey and send it to all your friends, or even a group of strangers, as a test group. They could try a quick demo of the app and provide you with near-immediate feedback. If you have a budget, you could use paid traffic to get unbiased feedback via social media. Through this process, there are three outcomes.

1. **The market is not interested in what you created.** If that is the case, you didn't venture much so it really isn't a huge loss. That's really the whole point of the MVP; minimum investment results in minimal loss. You also saved yourself lots of time and money by not going into any further detail.

2. **The market may be interested in something a bit different, and the feedback helps you change directions.** This is actually the most common outcome. Very rarely do you hit the nail right on the head with the first iteration. Instead, you use the insights gathered in this testing phase to make tweaks to the existing plans.

3. **You slam it out of the park right out of the gate and people love the idea.** This is rare, but it is still possible. In following the MVP strategy, you avoid wasting time and money on a bad idea and you receive useful feedback from your potential customers. Remember, your time and money are your most valuable resources, so you need to preserve them at all times.

How to Test an Idea

Here are my steps for testing an idea using the MVP approach:

1. Study the competition (something you will also do when determining your niche's quality bar).

2. Determine the simplest solution you can provide.

3. Create that solution (product, service, etc.) or create a landing page with a wait list for that future solution.

4. Share the solution with friends and family members for initial feedback.

5. Make necessary changes, if needed.

6. Share the solution with strangers, likely via the internet.

7. Assess feedback.

As far as solutions, don't reinvent the wheel. Your competitors are already providing solutions, so you can likely take what they are doing and potentially improve upon it. I looked at the videos that Jeremy from Financial Education and Jack Chapple were doing and emulated them, often covering the same topics as videos that did well for them. Once you come up with your MVP, the next step is to go out to the market and test it. If you are starting some type of service-based business, figure out what service you can offer people with minimal investment into equipment, ideally zero. If you think back to my lawn mowing business, I was able to get that off the ground borrowing the mower from my father.

After you come up with this idea, the next step is to spread the word. I'd like to dispel one of the most common business sayings out there that is totally false. The phrase "if you build it, they will come" doesn't apply to business, at least no longer today. Simply creating something good does not mean that people will magically come to find it. I have never found this to be the case across any business venture I have launched, nor have I observed this happening for others. Instead, you need to go out and gather the people. Don't wait for them to come—go and get them yourself. Use any tools at your disposal to get as many people testing out your MVP as possible.

At the end of the day, you have to be excited about your business. Feeling shy or embarrassed about your new business venture is unlikely to translate to success. It's perfectly normal to feel that way, as this is a limiting belief most of us have. Keep in mind where that feeling is coming from. Most people who are embarrassed of sharing their business with their peers are worried about being ridiculed or criticized. Whenever new ideas are introduced, you are almost certain to receive criticism. People who are within your circle are prone to either tell you exactly what you want to hear or criticize you for breaking out of the mold. You could have a perfectly good idea, but your peers may criticize it to discourage you from pursuing it. This is simply from the footing that they don't want to see you doing better than them. That is often why people will test online-based ideas with paid traffic.

Instead of gathering feedback from people with emotional ties to you, these are completely anonymous strangers who are going to give you 100 percent unbiased feedback.

My MVP Approach

I applied the MVP approach myself when I started recording videos in my car. I didn't start making a meaningful amount of money right out of the gate with my YouTube channel, but engagement was very important to me as well. This refers to the number of people who engage with your content by liking, subscribing, disliking, sharing, and commenting. Even though I didn't have a lot of followers at first, people were watching, liking, and commenting, and some were even subscribing. I had a feeling that money would eventually follow engagement, so I stayed positive and on track with my goals. Beyond my financial goals, once my channel was off the ground, I set goals for myself in terms of total views, likes, and subscribers. However, in order to reach these goals, I needed to follow a clear and well-defined strategy. I would fine-tune this strategy through the MVP approach.

After testing the market with my videos, I got feedback from the data I was seeing over the first month. Almost every video relating to nutrition, personal development, and fitness was doing poorly. Many had fewer than 10 views. However, the videos about investing and money were continuing to get views day after day. I had received valuable feedback from my MVP of short, low-production quality videos. Since views and other metrics were improving, I decided to invest a little bit more money into a better camera, lighting, and set. I already had a proven concept, so I felt like it was worth the investment now. I started exclusively making videos about topics related to money, finance, and investing. In addition, I started recording these videos in front of a whiteboard with somewhat professional lighting. This allowed me to write out a lot of the lessons I was looking to teach. Had I not tested this idea out first, it could have been a big mistake to dump a lot of money into production equipment. You don't need to go all in with every single idea.

Keep in mind that you won't always have success with your new offering to the world. This was the case with me when I was 17. I followed the MVP approach correctly; however, the feedback I received wasn't as positive as the previous example with my YouTube channel. I had decided to try out a business venture related to green energy after conducting a home energy audit for a school assignment. This involved going around and jotting down the wattages of all light bulbs, appliances, and other things that are plugged in. Based on this, I then had to estimate the total cost of energy usage and the overall cost savings of switching to the swirly CFL bulbs. Swapping out roughly 40 light bulbs in my house would result in an estimated cost saving of $30 a month. I did a trial run and asked my mom if I could swap the light bulbs. She was on board, so I went to Home Depot and grabbed a few boxes of bulbs. I then went through the house and swapped them all out. At that point, I had a light bulb go off in my head (pun intended).

I wondered if other people out there would be interested in having me do this as a service. Since there was a cost savings associated with the switch, I believed it would be easy to convince people to do it since it would pay for itself over time. The challenge would be clearly communicating that message with my potential customers. I wrote down a list of what I viewed as the 10 most common objections I would receive and came up with answers to them in order to be better prepared.

Once I felt I was ready, I posted some ads on Craigslist for free home energy audits. I also had good-quality business cards and flyers professionally made. I didn't get any bites from the ads. After a few days, I asked my mom if she could offer me any referrals. There was a nice woman who lived down the street from us, so she called her and gave her the heads-up that I would be stopping over. As it turned out, she wasn't interested in a free audit. She said she was somewhat independently wealthy, so the cost savings would not be a motivating factor. This was not something I had prepared for with my sales pitch or my list of common objections. However, she was interested in being more eco-friendly. Without the energy audit and cost savings analysis, I was suddenly trying to get this woman to pay me to change out her lightbulbs. When I showed her my pricing, she looked up and said, "How much is it to just buy the bulbs from you instead?" It was at that point that I realized most people would not see the value of having someone come change their light bulbs. I ended up selling her some bulbs for $0.50 over what I paid, earning $6 in the process on a dozen bulbs. In addition, she paid me $10 to fix a few things in her place, like plugging in a lamp behind her couch. I left her house $16 richer and a bit embarrassed overall. While I felt foolish about this idea at the time, it was a perfect example of testing out an MVP. My profits covered my gas and the cost of the bulbs. The 500 business cards may have put me at a small loss; those went in the trash. I certainly didn't slam it out of the park, but I gained valuable feedback in the process.

Don't Fall in Love with Ideas

While there are many benefits to following this MVP approach, the last one I want to cover for now is this. When people go all in with a business or product idea, they risk becoming completely infatuated with it. As they keep thinking about it more and more, they build out the idea further and ultimately fall in love with it. At that point, they are now mixing emotions with what should otherwise be a financial decision—does the market like what you have to offer? If I have learned anything when it comes to the stock market, it is that emotions and money do not mix well. We have all seen those people on *Shark Tank* who have pumped their life savings into a gadget or idea that isn't going anywhere. Some of these people may be sticking with it based on the sunk cost fallacy, which is when you continue an endeavor simply because you have sunk time or money into it. The sunk cost fallacy explains why people sink hundreds of thousands of dollars into bad business ideas, poor investments, or even gambling. Even though it would be most beneficial to stop, it's difficult to recognize that benefit when you have already invested a significant amount of time or money. The MVP strategy allows you to test ideas while keeping your emotions from getting involved. You can certainly become excited about your ideas, but don't make the mistake of entering into a state of delusion based on your emotional connection to these ideas.

Key Takeaways
- Instead of setting a goal of making $1,000 or more per month right out of the gate, go out and make your first $100. This is the mile that needs to be run before the marathon.
- The Minimum Viable Product (MVP) approach enables you to get the most feedback for the least amount of effort.
- Test your ideas quickly and cheaply by using what you have with you right now rather than investing in new materials or equipment. (For example, you can use your phone camera to make content before buying fancy video equipment.)
- Avoid becoming emotional about your ideas. People fall in love with bad ideas all the time, and this can leave you clinging to a losing venture or strategy.
- We are programmed to spend more money and commit more time to something that has already consumed a lot of both. Avoid this sunk cost fallacy.

- The saying "if you build it, they will come" doesn't apply to business today. Prepare to get loud about your business.
- When testing ideas, you may want to seek out feedback from strangers to ensure that it's unbiased.

Get Your First 100 Fans

Once you have the general concept of your side hustle down, it's time to become the key spokesperson for your business. As I mentioned previously, you have to be borderline annoying when making this announcement to the world. Simply put, be prepared to get loud about your new business. There is no better tool to accomplish this than social media. Whether we like it or not, social media is the driving force behind almost all businesses today. In certain cases, like my own, social media could form the foundation of your business itself. Either way, you need to gather attention, and the absolute best way to accomplish this is through social media.

Making Social Media Work for You

Making a website is essential for all businesses, and a lot of potential customers also use social media to research businesses. Therefore, it's important to have a good online presence on social media and your business website. This is especially true if your side hustle is geared toward younger people, as they are more likely to conduct research about a business on social media platforms like Instagram. However, you cannot rule out those who research businesses on Google. Those potential customers would land on your website after searching about you. Through social media, every small business has the potential to become a brand. With a business website as well, you can ensure you are available where anyone is looking for you.

For the last decade, social media has been used by business owners as a digital portfolio. This is where they share their best work. For example, a restaurant would showcase their food, while a landscaper would showcase their past projects. In recent years, the way business owners used social media has begun to change and evolve due to the explosion of the vertical video, which can be viewed without rotating your phone. Vertical videos make it possible for people to consume and digest content quickly, especially through apps like TikTok and its competitors, such as Instagram Reels and YouTube Shorts. Most creators leverage all three. Short vertical videos posted either on business social media pages or stories have allowed business-related content to flourish. I'm not necessarily talking about formal business lessons either. Instead, you can create documentary-style videos about being a business owner. Using this format, you can give people an inside look at the day-to-day of your side hustle operation. In turn, they will begin to care about you and your business, and maybe even support it.

For example, if your side hustle is to detail cars, you could take before-and-after videos or teach people about the best products for the job. Your goal with these short videos is to provide value to others and to take your audience behind the scenes. By sharing all of the special products used, you are indirectly showing people how much they need to buy themselves in order to replicate what you do. This could lead to them calling you for a detailing appointment rather than trying to do it themselves at home. People are naturally curious about what goes on within a small business. Use this new content medium as a way to share your side hustle, tap into existing demand, and get people to care about you. However, the content should not ask them to come support your business. Instead, by creating content and adding value, you will establish yourself as an expert in your given field and also build a brand. Before people support your business, you need to get them to care about you. The best way to do this is through content that offers viewers an emotional connection to your life, business, and potentially even outside interests you may have. It's important not to go too far out there, though. You don't need to share the backstory behind your dog's name, or the identical birthmark you have with your dad. All details should relate back to your business.

Another important factor to consider when establishing yourself on any social media platform is social proof—a psychological phenomenon in which people tend to copy the actions of others. Let me give you an example of this in action. If you stumble across a channel and see it has 100,000 subscribers, you will be more likely to subscribe since a lot of people already have before you. On the other hand, if you discover a channel with 82 subscribers, you might be less likely to subscribe. This is one of the many reasons why it is so hard to gain followers when you have very few to begin with. People will be skeptical of your content at first, based on the fact that you have no social proof behind it. Anyone who clicks on a video with fewer than 100 views is going to have low expectations, so they might not click at all. It is important to have realistic expectations about results before starting something, which is why I am sharing all of this with you. When you have a following, it's easier to grow a following. When you don't, it's a challenge, but something you can accomplish. It's not a realistic goal to grow 1,000 followers on a plat-form in a week if you only have 10 to begin with. If you already have 100,000 followers, we are now talking about another 1 percent joining the club, which is far more realistic. Knowing what to expect will keep you motivated, and you will be more likely to stick with things.

When you first start out, you will be facing many head-winds, including social proof, but others too. Be prepared to build your audience base one member at a time for the first few weeks or even months. What I have found over the years is growth on social media is very similar to investing. Early on, you are contributing small amounts of money and seeing very little growth. If you remain consistent, those small amounts earn dividends, allowing your money to grow—ideally with reinvestment of those dividends. If you keep contributing money and never stop investing, you will amass tremendous amounts of wealth in the long run. Those few followers you are growing day to day are similar to those small contributions early on to your investment portfolio. At the time, they seem meaningless. In the long run, they prove to be tremendously valuable. This is based on compounding, leading to exponential growth of both money and your audience.

The Snowball Effect

Compound interest and exponential growth are important concepts to grasp in life and in business. However, they both remain widely misunderstood. In an attempt to clear things up and explain this as simply as possible, I created a viral video sensation that served as a springboard for my audience growth. One of the first key lessons I taught on my YouTube channel was the concept of compound interest, often referred to as "the snowball effect." So what is compound interest? The best explanation I've heard is that compound interest is "interest earned on interest" or "dividends earned from dividends." Let's say you had $100 invested and you earned $5 over the course of a year paid out in dividends. If you put that $5 back into the stock that paid you dividends, you would now earn future dividends on that $5 investment for as long as you held onto it. If you repeat this over and over, the snowball effect takes place. Your money grows exponentially. If you need a refresh, that is one of those rounded line charts that starts off relatively consistent, but over time growth accelerates rapidly, sending the line upward. A linear growth chart (simple interest), over time, is the same growth rate forever. This would be a line chart heading upward at a 10-degree angle, for example. If you overlay these two graphs, they look nearly identical at first. It's only when you zoom out that you see the big difference.

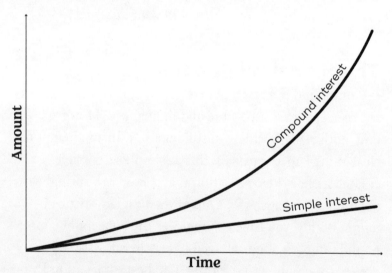

Simple interest grows at the same rate. Compound interest grows exponentially.

Why is called the snowball effect? If you grew up in a snowy climate, think back to making a snowman as a child. The very first step is to grab the biggest chunk of snow you can, often packing a mega-snowball between your gloves. After that, you start the exhaustive process of rolling it around on the ground. As an impatient child, you probably looked at the ball of snow and thought that it wasn't getting any larger. While some would give up at this point, those who kept rolling it around would eventually start seeing the ball of snow grow larger. Once it is big enough, it becomes easier to move and the snowball grows faster and faster with every push you make. By the end, you have a gigantic snowball, which should serve as an excellent base for your snowman. With the realization of how this process works, you rinse and repeat, building a series of snowballs for the different levels of your creation. This is precisely how compound interest works. It takes a lot of effort at first to get minimal results from rolling a small ball of snow around on your hands and knees, but it takes little effort to grow that ball of snow once it is knee high. What a lot of people do not realize is that the exponential growth associated with compound interest applies to growth in other areas outside of money, including social media. Starting off is basically the equivalent of packing that ball of snow and rolling it around on the ground. You won't see much in terms of results at first, but you have to be patient and keep going.

The growth of an audience online is exponential; it compounds over time. When I first started my YouTube channel, it took me to seven weeks to get 100 followers. If growth on social media was linear, that would mean my growth rate of 100 subscribers every seven weeks would continue like that over and over again. Based on that, over the last five years, I would have grown to a total of 3,724 subscribers. Instead, I have amassed a following of nearly 1,000,000 YouTube subscribers. That growth sounds super exciting, but it all starts with small, incremental progress. If you want to get to the point where you are gaining hundreds of followers per day, you have to start out by gaining just one follower a day. This is similar to someone earning $100 a day from their investment portfolio. They started with $1 a day and before that $0.10 a day. Think about this: every single piece of content you create has the possibility to earn you new followers. This is especially true on platforms like YouTube that have a lot of search traffic. If you only have one video gaining you one new subscriber a week, you will end up with 52 subscribers in a year. If you instead have 100 videos, each gaining you one new subscriber a week, you will end up with 5,200 subscribers. It is simply a numbers game, like many things in life. More content means more opportunities for views and subscribers. In addition, the consistent creation of content means you have more content each week gathering new followers, meaning your audience is growing faster every single week. It's often a combination of this and algorithms being in your favor that leads to the exponential growth of social media followers. A lot of algorithms won't share your content until you have been regularly creating content on the platform. This is especially true with blogging.

Google wants to see that you are well-established before they send traffic your way. Knowing this early on makes it far easier to stick it out, as you now know what to expect and the reasons behind it. Consistency is key.

Your Business Website

Before we get into my specific strategies for marketing yourself on social media, I want to provide more clarity on the website you will be creating for your business. As mentioned before, I am involved with multiple blogs. These are all self-hosted WordPress websites. We will touch on hosting more later in this chapter, but for now just think of it as a subscription that you pay in order to have your site available to the world. I use WordPress and host content myself because I want the greatest level of control and customization with my sites. However, this is also a more complicated website building process. If you are creating a content-based side hustle like me, it's a good idea to follow suit and create a self-hosted WordPress website. (I actually have a video on this over on YouTube, if you search for "Ryan Scribner WordPress" you will find it.) Keep in mind, there is a learning curve associated with this type of website. On the other hand, if you are simply creating a website as a means of exposure for your side hustle or business, you probably don't need a self-hosted WordPress site. Instead, here are simple tools to help you jump-start your website:

- **Beacons.ai:** This is a unique tool that helps you build a simple "link in bio" website. If you are looking for the easiest website option, you can put one of these sites together in minutes. Ready for the best part? It's free. I actually became an angel investor in this start-up after learning about it. I love companies like this that are capitalizing on the creator economy.

- **Wix:** While there are many site builders out there, Wix has a top spot on my list. Before switching to WordPress, the very first version of my website was built and hosted on Wix. You have a tremendous amount of flexibility with this platform as well as the ability to set up custom email inboxes using your domain name. There is a monthly subscription cost associated with Wix.

- **wordpress.com:** If you like the idea of WordPress but aren't ready to go all in, they have a simple site builder model that is similar to Wix. Instead of self-hosting your own site, you build a website on their platform. (If you are looking to create a self-hosted WordPress site, you want wordpress.org instead of wordpress.com.)

Marketing Yourself on Social Media

While social media is the best way to get a large audience to care about your side hustle, the act of posting content will not automatically garner a following. It's entirely possible to create content that people simply don't care about. According to Statista, as of February 2022, about 30,000 hours of content are uploaded to YouTube every hour. This figure is only expected to go up over time, as it has in prior years. Most of that content goes nowhere. I experienced this firsthand when I was making fitness and nutrition videos early on that got 10 views or less in the first month. I was among those in this statistic creating content that would rarely, if ever, see the light of day. The same is true for all social media platforms— there's a huge amount of content that falls into the abyss, while a small amount of the content does exceptionally well. It all comes back to supply and demand. If there is a high supply of content—think comedy channels or vlogs— it's extremely difficult to break out. On the other hand, if you were one of the first crypto channels during the Bitcoin run in 2017, you had a huge demand on your content out of nowhere, since there was almost no supply of content. Even if your business isn't centered around content creation, you need to know what type of content to create in order to market your business. By now, you should understand why this is a must for all businesses, both online and offline.

Here are my strategies for marketing yourself effectively on social media:

- **Vulnerability is power, so don't be afraid to open up.** Emotional connections make people care, and they need to care about you before they can care about your business. No, this doesn't mean being over the top. Instead, try to just be yourself. Keep in mind that everything should relate back to your business.

- **Share your story.** We all have one—it's what got you to this book! Why are you starting a side hustle?

This is usually a great place to share some vulnerability in the form of your emotional connection to your business venture.

- **Keep it quick.** Content today needs to hold attention well, especially with vertical video. I suggest writing down what you want to say, then eliminating as many words as possible before shooting a vertical video. On YouTube, this isn't the case as much. I follow a bulleted outline for those videos and a more off-the-cuff format.

- **Teach people things.** It doesn't matter if the information is useful or applicable to their lives. We all like to learn new things, so weave lessons into your content about whatever it is that you are doing. What would people like to know about your business or industry?

- **Stay on brand.** Once you determine the right quality bar for your content, and figure out your logo and other factors, you need to be consistent. For example, if you plan on using a ring light in your videos, you need to do this every single time, forever. Your audience will come to expect a certain level of quality, so you need to keep it there.

A great example of social media marketing comes from a candle maker named Raffi Arslanian. I stumbled across his TikTok page (@thompsonferrier_nyc) one day and followed him immediately after seeing his first video. He has a luxury candle brand based out of New York City but primarily sells high-end decorative candles online. On his page, Raffi shares the different aspects of his business. He shows his viewers both the ups and the downs, such as rising material costs for his supplies. Even though this might sound like a rather niche topic, he has grown to over 150,000 followers on TikTok. His bio has a direct link to his business website, where his audience can view and purchase his candles. The important thing is that his videos aren't saying, "Hey, go buy my candles." In fact, I don't even think he even mentions the website link. Instead, people become interested in who he is as a person and then naturally explore his business further. He's just providing free value on the internet for people, not pitching his product.

I don't know Raffi personally, but I will tell you that nothing he is doing here is by mistake. He knows exactly how to use social media and the vertical video as a massive growth catalyst for his business. You can no longer simply rely on foot traffic for sales if you have a brick-and-mortar business. If Raffi were simply selling candles out of his shop in NYC, he would not be doing nearly as well as he is by leveraging social media. Not to mention, lockdowns during the pandemic would have been detrimental to his business if he didn't have e-commerce to rely on. Those who want to jump-start their business should also consider adding vertical video, just like Raffi. You can even post the same content to multiple platforms such as TikTok, YouTube Shorts, Instagram Reels, and even LinkedIn to maximize exposure. You might think that it is going to be a lot of work, but all you will be doing is documenting things that are already happening. If you don't use social media for your business and your competitor does, they will have a massive advantage over you that grows larger over time. Things are becoming more digital and internet based over time.

Gaining Your First 100 Followers

There is a fine line between spreading the word about your business and going over the top and being annoying. To get your first 100 fans or followers, you want to be as close to that line as possible. In fact, I would rather see someone being annoying about their new business instead of secretive. In addition, you must be incredibly patient. You need to have reasonable expectations in order to stick it out.

Let's get into specific strategies for your first 100 followers.

1. HIT THE CELL

While I am a bit embarrassed about it now, at one point I was involved in a multi-level marketing (MLM) business. For those who aren't familiar, this is a direct-to-consumer sales opportunity in which you usually become a rep selling a product or service, but above all else, your goal is recruitment. The incentive is usually to earn a percentage of each person in your downline. This is a term in the MLM community used to label each person you refer to the business opportunity itself. Usually, you earn a percentage from the sales of each referral and potentially even from the referrals of your referral. There are countless MLMs out there such as Herbalife, Cutco, and Amway Global, to name a few. They all advertise very similar characteristics, promises, and outcomes. Few people have success with them, as they tend to be a very oversaturated opportunity with expensive or lousy products. Think low demand, high supply. Nonetheless, I did learn a few business lessons while I was involved with this venture. When you join an MLM, one of the first things you have to do is go through your phone contacts. You then make an exhaustive list of everyone you know, knew, or sort of knew—essentially, everyone in your contacts. The next step, at least for an MLM, is to reach out to all of these people. The goal is to either sell them some product or service, or better yet, enroll them in the business yourself.

What I recommend doing is following this exact strategy, minus the crappy MLM products. Instead, you will be sharing your MVP once you have created it. Again, you might do a smaller test group in the beginning when evaluating different ideas. However, after that, you need to leverage your entire personal network. At this point in time, you could ask all your contacts to follow you on social media. (Make sure you have some content up before asking people to follow you.) If you aren't planning to leverage social media, you could instead share what your MVP is and ask your contacts to spread the word. For example, if you decide to offer deck sealing as a side hustle, you spread the word about it. That could be as simple as sending a text saying "Hey! I am doing deck sealing now, so message me before I get too busy." You could then ask those who responded to spread the word. You will be very surprised by what people are willing to do to help you out. The key is to not be afraid to ask in the right manner. If done properly, you aren't trying to sell them anything at all. Instead, you're looking for support.

You should always give people a clear call to action about what you want them to do. For example, with the deck sealing scenario, the call to action was to respond to your message. One of the worst things you can do is leave everything completely open-ended. You cannot expect your audience to know what step they should take next if they want to support you. If you don't give people clear direction, the action most people will take is no action at all. Over the years, I have learned that you need to be as clear as possible when instructing someone on what you want them to do. Your best bet is likely to ask them to follow you or subscribe to your various social media platforms.

2. THE COLD DM

Once you have exhausted your contacts list, you should have a few followers on your different social media platforms. Believe it or not, this gives you some small level of social proof already. The next strategy you could deploy is interacting with strangers to spread awareness about your business. This isn't an essential strategy by any means, and there are probably better uses of your time. However, you could keep this in your back pocket for when you are standing in line at the grocery store. If you follow my recommendation from earlier about auditing your time, you'll likely be surprised with how much idle time you have throughout the day. I'm always looking to double down on what would have ordinarily been wasted time. If you're already stuck doing nothing, why not respond to random messages on Instagram?

Here's what this looked like for me in 2016. When I first posted content on YouTube, I uploaded about 50 videos all at once. I then shared many of them on social media. After that, I sent a Facebook message to every one of my close friends and family members and asked them to subscribe to my channel. This got me about 20 fans right out of the gate. After that, it was an exhaustive process of just engaging with strangers online and building an audience one person at a time. I would follow random people on Twitter (if doing this today, I would use Instagram) and send direct messages to the ones that would follow me back. I would follow about 50 people a day, and roughly 40 percent of them would follow me back. After that, I would message those 20 or so people and start a conversation. Roughly 50 percent of them would respond, leaving me communicating with about 10 strangers a day. At some point in the conversation, I would organically mention my channel when it seemed to fit. Based on that, I would get one or two people to subscribe each day.

I repeated this process almost every single day. Even so, it took me just over seven weeks to get 100 subscribers on YouTube. It's a matter of reaching out to friends, asking for favors, and maybe even reaching out to strangers (as long as you do so safely). Keep in mind that when I was doing this, I was spending three to four hours a day at my desk at work with almost nothing else to do. This was also back in 2016, and some of these practices are now against the terms of service for many social media platforms. In a nutshell, be strategic and don't overdo it. Following hundreds of accounts out of nowhere can get you banned on many platforms, so use your time wisely and engage with the ones that seem most relevant or useful.

3. BECOME A QUORA KNOW-IT-ALL

This is what I believe to be one of the most under-utilized sources of new followers or leads for your side hustle. As a kid, I spent a lot of time on Yahoo Answers. This was a predecessor to Quora, although it is no longer around today. Both of these sites are essentially platforms where people ask questions and other experts on the site answer them. The answers that get the most upvotes rise to the top. What is interesting about this is that a lot of these questions being asked end up ranking for Google searches around the term. For example, if someone asks about losing weight with apple cider vinegar on Quora, the thread is likely to show up as a Google result for searches related to "apple cider vinegar to weight loss." Thus far at least, the Google algorithm really likes these user-generated answer sites. With Quora, you are able to include hyperlinks in your answers and provide your website and social media links in your bio. Quora could be used to drum up leads for an online service-based business or to get some initial traffic over to a blog. While I haven't personally used Quora for lead generation, I know many people who have successfully done so.

Let's say you're starting an online service-based side hustle offering help with WordPress. Essentially, you would start off by marketing your skills with your own website and social media. Then, in your Quora bio, you could include information about your business and links to your website and social media. After that, you can specifically search and follow categories. You could follow categories like "Websites" or "WordPress" and then pop on to answer questions once or twice a day. The goal here isn't to market your services. The goal is to simply provide free value to others. People will naturally find that information when they click on your profile. Some of the top people on Quora get millions of views on their answers every single month.

4. SEARCH-BASED CONTENT STRATEGY

This is something I had to learn after a few frustrating months spent creating content that nobody watched. Sure, some of my videos did well. However, most of them were complete duds. When I discussed this with my cousin Ben, he asked me if people were actually searching for the topics I'd do my videos on. I told him that I really had no idea. One of my videos discussed the health benefits of almonds and avocados. Although I was knowledgeable about that topic at the time, it didn't necessarily mean people were looking for that information. I realized that I had been following a sort of a backward approach to my content. I was simply making videos about topics I was interested in and knowledgeable of. Then I would post the videos and hope there was an audience for them. I should have done the opposite instead. You want to be sure there is an audience for the content before spending your time. Then you can apply this approach as part of your overall content strategy.

Through this strategy, you provide what people are searching for in the first place. The easiest and most effective way to apply this strategy is to use auto-suggested terms on Google, YouTube, or other search-based platforms. Simply type in a keyword related to your niche and see what Google suggests around it. Then play around with it by adding different letters before or after that word and seeing what Google suggests. Generally speaking, the longer a search term is in word count, the less competitive it is. In the SEO (search engine optimization) world, this is referred to as a "long-tail" keyword. This is a longer, more specific search term. "Short-tail" keywords, on the other hand, are three words or less. These are broader, more popular searches.

Here's an example using the topic of dividend investing:

- Short-tail keyword: "Dividend stocks"
- Long-tail keyword: "How to tell when a stock will pay the next dividend"

The short-tail search terms are going to be far more competitive. Your goal should be to break into these results over time, not right out of the gate. Beginners should instead focus on these long-tail keywords, as they are far less competitive in most niches. We grew Investing Simple by solely focusing on these lower-competition articles being overlooked by the big players. The gist of this strategy is to create content around things people were already searching.

5. GRASSROOTS MARKETING

Do not overlook grassroots marketing. Grassroots marketing involves spreading the word about your business in the real world. You know, actual human-to-human interaction. We tend to forget that our followers are real people. Don't be afraid to order a stack of business cards and hit the pavement. You could head out to a local concert, park, or venue and talk to new people. In this day and age, you need to be aware of any social distancing limitations or things of that nature beforehand. However, this is a great strategy that is overlooked by many.

Keep in mind, the goal of grassroots marketing is not to get someone to buy your product then and there. You don't want to be one of those people approaching strangers in a parking lot trying to sell them a wallet. Instead, you are just getting to know people, making friends, and sharing information about your side hustle. I've helped many people with strategies like this, and it can actually be a lot of fun. Many years ago, I helped one of my friends by asking strangers at a mall to check out his band's music. We ended up getting almost 20 followers in a single day.

Because your first 100 followers are truly earned one at a time, this was a significant number.

Beyond the first 100, you should make sure that the people following you actually care about your content. Engagement is an important metric for almost all social media platforms. Your content might not do well if your followers aren't interested. You may want to be in a certain place today with your social media accounts. Maybe your goal is to have 1,000 followers. I want to remind you to remain patient and build things correctly. It's never a good idea to go out and buy followers for your social media profiles. This leads to you having a bunch of fake, inactive followers who don't engage with your content. This low engagement can signal to the algorithm that your content is lousy, leading to you becoming shadow banned. This is when no matter what you post, your content gets a consistently low amount of engagement. There is no shortcut, hack, or gimmick. Simply remain consistent.

Key Takeaways

- You need to spread the word about your venture, and the best way to do this is through social media. The side hustle starter pack is a website and an Instagram page.
- Consider documenting your side hustle journey through short vertical videos. You can post the same content to multiple platforms, allowing you to maximize reach and exposure.

- Before asking people to support you, try to provide value to them in some way. The best way to do this is by simply teaching people interesting things about what you do.

- The same exponential growth associated with compounding financial returns applies to audience growth on social media. The more content you post, the more content you have out there to potentially gain you new followers.

- Sharing your story with your audience is a great way to build an emotional connection. However, you need to keep it concise. Consider writing out what you plan on saying first, then reducing it to as few words as possible.

- Make sure there is demand or an audience before creating content. This can be accomplished through basic research of online search terms.

- Don't underestimate grassroots marketing. Remember, your potential followers are real people walking around in the world today.

From Side Hustle to Main Hustle

Let's revisit childhood business lessons, as these are often the most important in life. As a kid, you may have started a business as a means of making some extra money, like me with my lawn mowing gig. One of the most common examples of this is a lemonade stand. (Side note: please support children doing this! A lemonade stand is a great stepping stone into entrepreneurship.) Let's say you have a lemonade stand and you end up making $20 after a day. After factoring in the cost for sugar and lemons, you realized a profit of $17. While that is a decent chunk of change for a kid, maybe you are a bit more ambitious. The next morning, you decide to open four stands instead of one, recruiting the neighbor kids. In return, your will pay them each $5 to monitor the stand. If all four stands profit $17 like the one did yesterday, you will make $12 per stand after paying your helpers, or $48 total.

During the first hour of the day, things are running smoothly. However, by noon, chaos ensues. One of the stands got swarmed and is completely out of lemons. Now, you are riding your bike over to the grocery store. As you are on your way, you get a call from your friend at stand 3. He quits, walking away with the $5. Now you are scrambling for more lemons, while trying to find someone else to work. After getting the lemons, you drop them off and head over to the empty stand to operate it yourself. Problems like this repeat throughout the day. By the end, you find you only managed to bring in $50 of total revenue. As it turned out, there wasn't enough demand for all four stands to do as well as the singular one, as neighbors were willing to walk. After paying your helpers, including the one who walked off the job, you have $30 left. Unfortunately, you way overbought on the lemons and sugar based on the volume of sales you did with the first stand. As a result, you have a ton of extra sugar and lemons. This ended up costing you $12, leaving you with $18 profit.

In this scenario, you just went from a simple-to-operate business (one lemonade stand that profited $17) to a complicated one (four stands that only profited one single dollar more). What happened? As it turns out, the business of operating lemonade stands is one that is difficult to scale. The best way to understand this is to think of businesses as machines. The businesses that scale more easily are well-oiled machines that don't break down much. Businesses that are difficult to scale are machines that need constant repair and maintenance. On a routine basis, everything screeches to a halt. It's like driving a vehicle that breaks down all the time. You simply cannot rely on it. You want to become aware of what type of machine you are working with. In the lemonade stand example, this would be an unreliable machine, in constant need of maintenance and attention. Ideally, you would want to find a more reliable machine, or an easier-to-scale business venture. However, understand that there's no such thing as a business that is easy to scale. Scaling won't happen overnight. In my case with my YouTube channel, I had to not only scale my audience, but also my revenue. What I found is that there was quite a lot of overlap with the strategies involved with both. The first major catalyst that kicked off my growth, and thus led to me scaling the business, was a single video I posted back in July of 2017.

My First Viral Video

My first viral video, the one about compound interest and becoming a millionaire, took me from 10,000 YouTube subscribers to over 40,000 in just a few weeks. I was making hundreds of dollars a day in ad revenue while the video was taking off. This was unheard of; prior to the video going viral, I was making $50 a day at best. In addition, this was one of the first viral pieces of content in the financial niche on YouTube. I was convinced that this one video was going to be my ticket to making unlimited amounts of money on YouTube. I was simply going to copy and paste the strategies, creating viral video after viral video. Despite the early win, I soon ran into multiple problems with this strategy. The main problem was that a viral video is not a repeatable outcome. In fact, it is largely based on luck. The video that went viral had a very catchy hook. But here's the problem: it's not easy to find an angle out there like this for every single important financial concept. Over the next few months, I tried to copy and paste this viral video strategy at least 20 times with no success. It was a very frustrating process, because I would end up spending an entire day or two planning everything out. This included an enticing thumbnail, a catchy title, and what I thought to be exceptional content that hooked the audience immediately. But I soon realized that viral content is mostly random.

Today, I have probably created over a thousand videos and written hundreds of articles. What I can tell you with certainty is that viral videos are not a predictable outcome. You create a viral video by creating your very best content, not by having this goal of creating a viral video. Think about Netflix with hit shows like *Tiger King*. They didn't go out to zoos with the goal of creating a record-breaking documentary and a global phenomenon. Instead, they put their best foot forward, consistently, over time. Viral content is a by-product of wonderful content, not something you can go after individually. As a result, you can't rely on viral videos to generate steady income or viewership. Any benefit derived from viral content needs to be looked at as a bonus. It's certainly exciting when it happens, and it can make you a lot of money overnight, but it can't be relied on.

A One-Legged Stool

After many months of trying to recreate a viral video with no success, I realized I had to find other revenue streams. The problem was, I was essentially sitting on a one-legged stool. I was relying on one income stream, when the average millionaire has seven or more. I knew I needed to add more legs to my stool in order to better support myself. The channel was bringing in about $3,000 a month at this point, but I was running around like a chicken with my head cut off. I was posting videos five times a week, and spending almost the entirety of every day working on something related to my brand or my channel. On weekends, I was often so stressed out about my business that I couldn't even enjoy time spent with friends and family without worrying about things in the back of my mind. I could have sustained myself on $3,000 monthly, but the work that I was doing would not be sustainable for long. Not to mention, I wasn't in this to simply make a few thousand a month. I had much bigger goals. For now, I needed to figure out how to move the needle and make more money with less activity.

I was learning how to diversify my revenue streams through self-education. However, I didn't necessarily pick the right opportunities at first. It's rare that you do with any business, which is why you have to constantly adapt.

Following the advice of *Rich Dad, Poor Dad*, I had multiple personal income streams at the time, including my channel and stocks. However, my business itself did not have diversified revenue streams. I was selling an e-book at the time, but that was only generating a few hundred dollars in revenue monthly. In addition, Amazon affiliate links earned me around $100 monthly. I had the right ideas in mind, but I was not focused on diversification nearly enough. Over 95 percent of my income at the time was coming from one source, YouTube ads. The only other source, Amazon affiliate links, was a negligible amount of money. It was pretty much the definition of having all of your eggs in one basket, then moving one single egg to your second basket. This needed to change.

Digital Courses and Membership Sites

I decided to start exploring what my peers were doing on YouTube to make money. Perhaps they had come up with multiple income streams for their channels? No need to reinvent the wheel. I noticed that one of my mentors, Jordan, had a course on Fulfillment by Amazon (FBA). (This is a business model in which you sell products on Amazon that you have purchased from a supplier, typically overseas. You serve as the middleman, making money on the markup.) I asked Jordan if he sold many copies of his course, since it was rather expensive at $697. I was astonished when he told me he was selling multiple copies of the course every single day. At that point, I asked him if he thought I should do something similar related to investing and he was fully supportive of the idea. I was convinced I had the second leg to my stool, so I went all in. Over the next few months, I ended up creating my own 12-hour course on stock market investing. This was a massive undertaking, as I was creating the course content and then recording and editing the lectures while simultaneously posting five videos a week on my channel.

After a few weeks of this, I ended up completely crashing and almost gave up on the project. I had spent over 100 hours and I was only about 70 percent done. I circled back to Jordan, and he gave me a wonderful idea. Based on his advice, what I decided to do was launch the course early and stagger out the release of the content. I knew that some money in my pocket would motivate me to finish the project, and I wasn't wrong.

I ended up launching the course to my email list, which had around 10,000 subscribers at the time. The price tag was a little lower than Jordan's, at $497. I made over $7,000 on the first day. While this may not seem like a lot to some, this wildly exceeded my expectations. I was convinced I was sitting on a gold mine, soon to be earning thousands of dollars passively every single week. The addition of this online course to my overall revenue portfolio did help, but it wasn't a reliable revenue stream. I had my first month where I made over $10,000 when I launched the course, but after that it was all over the place.

Some months I would sell two copies of the course, others I would sell 10. It was entirely unpredictable. While it wasn't as stressful as relying on repeat viral videos as an income source, it was still not something I could count on.

This eventually led me to create a membership site instead. My goal at the time was to find a somewhat predictable monthly passive income source. I decided to start a stock analysis subscription service called Stock Radar at a cost of $19 per month. This was in early 2018, a few months after I had launched and finished the course. When I initially launched the membership site, the stock market was going up consistently, so people were very interested in my stock analysis. I was able to build up the membership site to a few hundred members in no time at all.

Membership Churn Rate

Things were going well with this site for a few months, but then the market began to turn around. As soon as the stock market stopped going up week after week, interest in new stock picks or analysis dwindled significantly. That was when I learned about something called *membership churn*. This refers to the number of members you end up losing versus gaining. In an ideal scenario, you are increasing your new members more quickly than your existing members are canceling. Unfortunately, I had found myself in the exact opposite situation. I had more members canceling monthly than I had signing up. After a few failed marketing efforts to replenish the membership site, I sat down and ran the numbers to see how bad things were. At the peak, I had brought in $6,000 of monthly recurring revenue. However, this was taking up about 30 percent of the time I was spending working. I was losing 30 members more per month than I was gaining.

The main problem was the fact that I was charging $19 per month. It was too expensive for most people, and those who were not using it were likely to cancel. Based on this membership churn, my monthly recurring revenue was on the road to decline by about $500 every single month. I kept things going for a few months longer, but I pulled the plug when I dropped below 200 members. I cancelled the site and all subscriptions thereafter. I had just spent the last year spinning my tires in the mud. The stock market course had mixed results. The membership site did well at first, but ultimately the high churn made it a losing business venture for me. I share this both in the spirit of authenticity as well as to demonstrate that success does not happen in a straight line. You can spend a year (or even longer) focusing on the wrong things, and still do well in the long run. While it is possible to have a thriving membership site, I was not successful with my first shot at it.

The only real way to make predictable revenue from online courses is to run paid ads, which was something I didn't want to do at the time. For many reasons, this is no longer a major component of my businesses today. Instead, I mostly provide free value rather than gated content people must pay to access. Many of the lectures from the stock market course I created years ago are now available on my YouTube channel for free. (Just search for "Ryan Scribner Stock Market Course.") I do still sell a course on affiliate marketing with an introduction lecture from my mentor Jake Woodard, but sales of digital courses account for a very small part of my total revenue today.

Listening to My Audience

After exhausting most other opportunities, I went back to the drawing board. I had spent hundreds of hours on a course and membership site, as well as multiple failed attempts at viral videos. While I hadn't slammed it out of the park, I did scale my income from $3,000 monthly to $10,000 during this time frame. Even though the course wasn't consistent, it was making me over $1,000 every month. In addition, my audience base and viewership were growing. Ad rates were going up too, meaning I made more money from the ads that ran on my content. Some people would be happy to bring in $10,000 per month from their business, but I knew there was the potential to do more. I was also scrambling and working around the clock in order to make that money. It was the opposite of passive income. I didn't quit my job to just to get by; I wanted to grow this channel into a thriving business. Beyond that, I needed to make sure this business allowed me to be able to step away from it and take a break, which was not the case with my current operation. I decided to turn to my audience for help.

At the time, I was getting tons of requests from my audience to do reviews of different financial apps like Robinhood and M1 Finance. I reached out to these companies to see if they had any type of affiliate or referral program. I started with a few reviews with the affiliate link in the description. Since there was high demand for this content and I was the first one making videos reviewing most of these apps, I struck gold. Within the first month of doing this, I had an income source of over $1,000 per month across all these affiliates from a small handful of videos. I was in disbelief, because making these videos didn't take much time compared to the hundreds of hours I was putting in on other projects. In no time at all, I had a new and significant revenue stream accounting for roughly 10 percent of my business income. In addition, this was far more predictable and consistent compared to online course sales, membership churn, and trying to create viral content.

I had a major paradigm shift at this point in terms of how I was going to monetize my content. Prior to this, I had tried to create catchy videos that would go viral in order to make money from the ads. Then I had tried to get my audience to watch my content by plugging my course with the hopes of then selling my own digital products to them. Now I was creating targeted content geared toward a specific audience. There was existing demand out there for reviews of financial apps. I was simply providing YouTube with content to fill the need. I was also able to monetize this as effectively as possible by establishing relationships with the brands.

Qualities of a Scalable Side Hustle

My YouTube channel was now diversified across ad revenue, course sales, and affiliate revenue. While I had three legs to my stool, I was worried about the stool itself. What if my YouTube channel was suddenly shut down, based on forces outside of my control? I wanted to make sure I had multiple stools, not just one. I knew I needed another separate business venture. After solely focusing on video content, I made a major diversification move in 2018 with the launch of my first investing blog, Investing Simple.

I had spent two years creating videos, but I was hitting some major roadblocks in terms of scaling. The main one was the fact that I was the only person who could create video content. However, this is not the case with a blog, since there could be an endless number of authors on the site. A significant difference between Investing Simple and my YouTube channel business is that I brought on a business partner. I knew that there would be a lot of work involved with getting another business off the ground, especially while I was still working on my channel full-time. I reached out to one of my high school friends, Ed Canty, who has a traditional background in finance. He works as a wealth advisor and has since become a Certified Financial Planner. We met for pizza, and I pitched him the idea for a finance blog. While Ed and I both spent years writing content for the site early on, we have since hired many talented freelance writers, so the content is handled by them. This means we can easily increase our content output by simply adding and training new writers. In addition, we have figured out a somewhat refined strategy for article topics based on SEO research. This means we have a general idea of whether we will be able to rank for a search term before creating the content. Sure, no business model is without hurdles to jump. While it isn't perfect, as no business model is, I have personally found blogging to be a highly scalable business. This led me to launching a second blog in 2020, Farmland Riches. This blog relates to the prospects of farmland investing, as well as review and comparison content related to the top farmland investing platforms. I also operate my personal brand website, ryanoscribner.com, as well as a rowing exercise site, rowingbasics.com. (This site is currently something I work on for fun with a few partners, but I do plan on monetizing it in the future.)

Why was blogging such an appealing business model for me? It has to do with the scalability. When it comes to scaling, I now consider the following:

- **Standalone brand:** This needs to be a business with a brand behind it, like Farmland Riches or Investing Simple. While I created the Farmland Riches brand, I actually purchased the Investing Simple brand, as it was tied to an Instagram page I bought in 2018. After pigeonholing myself with my personal channel, I learned the value of having numerous people creating content, as opposed to just one.

- **Contractor-based workforce:** Personally, I don't like opportunities that require full-time employees. Such opportunities hold many added layers of complication, like payroll and insurance. Unless you want to be your own mini-HR department, it's probably best for you to avoid these too, at least for your first side hustle.

- **Low overhead:** Overhead refers to the ongoing costs associated with running a business. I look for this number to be as low as possible, as this allows you to sustain yourself if revenue declines. Maintaining a low overhead is why I started my side hustle from my car, then transitioned to my mom's spare bedroom. Overhead includes costs such as office rent, utilities, subscriptions, mileage, etc.

- **Zero inventory:** I think there's enough to offer people in terms of a digital experience, whether that is content or an app or something else entirely. Keep in mind that as soon as you involve inventory, you also involve tons of complications such as mailing costs and handling returns.

- **Zero customer service:** I spent years working with the general public. While I love talking to people, I don't like any customer service–related tasks in my business. That's one of the other annoyances I ran into operating my membership site. The weekly "I forgot my password" emails were becoming too much. I wasn't big enough to justify hiring someone for customer service either, so it all fell on my shoulders.

- **Prevailing trend:** In the stock market, there is a saying that the trend is your friend. You can also follow this in business by jumping on growing opportunities. You can find out about trends by consuming the right kinds of content. I read publications like *The Wall Street Journal* and I watched other YouTube channels to see what topics did well for them.

- **Partnerships:** While they don't always end well, blogs are a good business to consider if you are looking to partner with someone or a few people. There are a lot of tasks involved, ranging from content to editorial to bookkeeping. All of my blogs have multiple partners, each bringing a different benefit to the operation.

Should YOU Quit Your Job?

This act of scaling up your side hustle often comes with a difficult, life-changing decision of whether to stay at your full-time job. Scaling your business is going to involve a huge time commitment, especially at the onset. You're likely to make a lot of mistakes and go through multiple business strategies like I did. Scaling your side hustle is an all-hands-on-deck scenario. You should be fully dedicated to something if you are really trying to go big with it. It would be difficult to accomplish this while working most jobs out there, but not impossible.

So when is the right time to quit? For some, that answer is never. If you like your job, simply supplement your income with your side hustle. Maybe this enables you to stash money away for retirement and take a few vacations each year. On the other hand, if you are like me and are using your side hustle as a means of escape, you probably want to get out sooner. In my opinion, quitting your day job should not even be considered as an option until you are making at least $2,000 in profit monthly from your side hustle. The thought process behind this is that most people are going to spend around 10 to 15 hours per week on their side hustle. If you are able to make $2,000 spending that amount of time on it, you should be able to make three to four times that by dedicating your efforts toward the venture full-time. If you aren't making $2,000 in profit monthly yet, you may not even have a viable side hustle. I recommend giving it more time while focusing on it as a side hustle, not a main business. Keep in mind that this is my recommendation on the earliest point at which to make this transition. You'll be far better off waiting until that number is larger, maybe even $5,000 to $10,000.

Remember what we covered earlier about business decisions and emotions? The decision to transition from a side hustle while working a job to focusing on your venture full-time should be strictly finance-based. I know you are probably excited to do it, but taking this jump at the wrong time could be detrimental to your success. I was truly not prepared for the amount of stress that taking the jump put me under. The right time to leave your main hustle is when you have prepared yourself financially and shown proof of concept with many months of earning thousands of dollars. Many people want to make the jump only to find that they don't have a parachute. This may not be the answer most people want to hear, but you do not want to mix in the added stress of having no income when you are still getting things off the ground.

Test, Learn, Adapt, Repeat

It took me about two years of trial and error to figure out what I was doing with my content-based business. Eventually, it led me to affiliate marketing as a primary focus. In the future, it will likely be something else. This is what a typical path looks like when you are building and then scaling a side hustle. You end up testing out a lot of different things, many of which won't work out as planned. In fact, you should think of these tests as individual MVPs.

Over the years, many have asked me what the secret is to having success with a side hustle. There is no secret! The most important action to creating a successful business is actually quite simple: keep moving and keep adapting. In my case, each idea was a building block for the next. With each change in my business model, I got closer and closer to a relatively consistent passive income stream to supplement YouTube ad revenue. People often go wrong when they cling to a certain idea. For example, when I had my first viral video on compound interest, I went down a rabbit hole trying to duplicate the outcome.

You do have to be patient with ideas and give them time, but on the other hand, you also have to know when to move on. Don't fall in love with a business idea, because it can lead to emotional decision-making. You have to consider that success does not happen in a straight line. There wasn't really any big break for me. Instead, it was a cycle of staying consistent. This, at the end of the day, is how you scale a business. It is a simple strategy of repeating a process in which the outcome is mostly predictable.

Key Takeaways

- Scaling is the process of turning a smaller operation into a larger one. This is often the point where your side hustle becomes a full-blown business.

- During the time of scaling, you will likely find yourself testing out new MVPs. When you find one or a few that work, see if you can replicate the results on a larger scale.

- Not all successful strategies will scale, because the phenomenon that led to success could be completely random.

- You probably won't have a "big break." Instead, long-term consistency and correct adaptation will lead to somewhat predictable results.

- The decision to pursue a side hustle full-time should be strictly based on finances.

- You don't have to scale your business. A bigger side hustle operation isn't always better than a small one.

- Your business needs multiple income streams, like the three legs on a stool. Without them, you are unstable.

Hedge, Hedge, Hedge

Once you have established your side hustle, meaning you have things up and running, it's time to begin safeguarding yourself and your business against potential bumps in the road. For most of these problems, it is a matter of when, not if, they will happen. For example, the inevitable data breach that involves your customer data. Or that password you use for everything gets compromised, which leads to you losing access to your social media profiles. You need to plan ahead for these things now so that you can protect yourself. This is done through a process called hedging. *Hedging* is a risk management strategy that safeguards against a potential negative outcome. It's a term most often used in the financial community; however, it applies to other areas of life too.

I first learned about hedging when I was a kid growing up in snowy upstate New York. When we were in elementary school, my siblings and I would perform all sorts of rituals to bring about a snow day from school. Once, after flushing ice cubes down the toilet and wearing my pajamas to bed inside out, I asked my dad if he thought that school would be closed the following day. His response was "Hope for the best, prepare for the worst." Although I didn't like his advice at the time, he was teaching me the valuable lesson of hedging. If school was closed the following morning, I would be able to skip doing my homework for one day and complete it during the snow day. But my dad encouraged me to hedge and prepare for the worst by doing my homework the night before, regardless. This way, my homework would be done if school didn't close. However, if the ice cubes and pajamas did the trick and school did close, I would have a full day without homework. While my friends would be stuck inside doing homework on snow days, I'd be out sledding and playing in the snow. As I got older, I learned how to apply the strategy of hedging to my professional decisions as well as personal investments.

Once you become aware of the concept of hedging, the next question you have to consider is how to hedge. Hedging allows you to protect yourself from a specific outcome. But how do you know what to protect yourself from in the first place? Since most of us do not have a crystal ball that can see into the future, we must rely on other information sources. The best source of information I have found is looking at what is going on in the world around you. This could mean *qualitative research*, making observations about life as you yourself interact with it. Or this could mean *quantitative research*, looking at hard numbers and data to predict future events or outcomes. In most cases, a combination of both works best. By following a combination of real-world observations and hard numbers, I have successfully hedged for many outcomes and navigated some challenging times. You can do exactly the same thing. It all starts with paying attention to what is going on around you.

Trends and Fads 101

The first step to hedging is identifying a trend. This will help you identify what you are protecting yourself from, and it may even give you an opportunity to make some money.

For example, during the early stages of the global pandemic in 2020, some who had tremendous foresight into situations properly hedged their portfolios, personal needs, or even businesses. By seeing the "writing on the wall," or evidence around them, they were able to make an assumption about what would happen in the future. Then they simply prepared themselves for this. As you can now see, it all starts with seeing the trends.

There are three different types of trends:

1. **A mega-trend:** This is a major movement that takes place over the span of many decades. For example, a current mega-trend is the boom in

senior housing. When I was searching for a side hustle, I realized that there was a mega-trend that I could capitalize on: the shift away from traditional media consumption toward user-generated content like YouTube.

2. **A trend:** While a mega-trend takes place over many decades, a trend develops over the course of a few years. However, a trend has the potential to turn into a mega-trend. One such example is juicing. While the concept has been around for centuries, interest in fruit and vegetable juice has skyrocketed in recent years. I've seen new juice shops opening up left and right all over the country. If people keep sustaining the trend, it has the potential to turn into a mega-trend.

3. **A fad:** A fad is something that becomes a social phenomenon out of nowhere and disappears just as quickly as it emerges. Some examples include planking, fidget spinners, and silly bands. Through social media, fads can now spread like wildfire on the Internet. You can ride the tidal wave of a fad to grow your business, but you can't expect the fad to keep going indefinitely. I learned this firsthand in 2016, when I sunk $100 on a fidget spinner review channel. While the channel received some hits initially, it ended up being a complete flop when the fad came to a crashing halt.

Now that you understand the differences between these, you need to consider how or if you respond to these different situations. More often than not, you will see someone making a knee-jerk reaction to something, which goes hand in hand with impulsive decision-making. For example, if you operate a mall kiosk, you might put thousands of dollars into fad products that will be a huge burden when demand collapses. Even if you sell out, you would be taking a gamble by reordering more inventory, as you could end up stuck holding onto it. How do you know when to stop ordering more and move on?

The analogy of sailing can be helpful in thinking about how you respond to these changing tides (pun intended). A fad is like a breeze on the water. You can adjust your sails to take advantage of it, allowing it to move you forward on your journey across the water. What you can't do is rely on it. That is because breezes come and go, changing directions at will. A trend is like the direction of the wind. It is relatively consistent—until there is a storm, of course. This is a force that you can rely in to propel yourself forward. However, wind alone isn't enough to get you moving. You need one final force, which is the current.

In sailing, it is the combination of the air around the boat working with the sails and the water underneath interacting with the boat components that move things along. Ocean currents are continuous and predictable, meaning they can be relied on too. A mega-trend is like the direction of the current. By following the trends and mega-trends that impact you, they become the forces that get you to where you want to be, just like the wind and the current when sailing. Fads can be used to speed up the process if you wish. What you cannot do is derail the entire course of your trip chasing a fad, or a short-lived breeze. This could leave you stranded.

A House on Sand Pillars

People often think that trends will never come to an end. However, that's not possible, as they always do. It's a preprogrammed human behavior to think this way. We tend to expect recent events happening right now to continue forever, something called the *familiarity effect*. Even mega-trends come to an end eventually. If you hold the false belief that whatever trend you are capitalizing on will last forever, you will get blindsided by reality at some point. Think about how Blockbuster had the opportunity to change gears and do video kiosk rentals like Redbox or offer web-based services like Netflix. They even, famously, had the opportunity to buy Netflix at one point. Instead, they believed the retail home video rental trend would keep going forever. We all know how that turned out. They went from thousands of stores to just one left operating as of 2022.

So how do you avoid falling into this familiarity bias? First, you must acknowledge that it's a false belief system. Once you realize that no trend lasts forever, it simply comes down to adaptation. I have experienced some major disruptions across my different businesses due to fluctuating trends. At the end of 2019, I became an affiliate for Airbnb. I listed my own bedroom, hosted guests, and documented the experience on my channel. The videos ended up doing quite well and quickly became a substantial affiliate revenue stream. I was soon earning over $3,000 per month. But then something happened that no one anticipated—the global pandemic hit. Within a week, Airbnb completely shuttered their affiliate program. At the time, I was frustrated. I thought that I would be earning a few thousand per month for years to follow. In addition, I was supposed to receive a big bonus once I hit 100 host referrals. All of that vanished. In 2022, we had another major affiliate "rug pull" with Coinbase. After spending months and thousands of dollars on resources for Investing Simple related to this crypto exchange, they halted their affiliate program overnight.

Disruptions like this happen, and they happen all the time in the world of business. They may not be as large in scale as a global pandemic, but they are unavoidable for the most part. Most of us have regular jobs that are very consistent, making this unfamiliar territory. We pretty much assume that if we follow the rules and meet expectations, we can rely on a weekly paycheck. While this is mostly true in the world of being an employee, this thought process needs to go out the window when becoming an entrepreneur. You may be receiving a consistent paycheck, but that doesn't mean your boss is making a consistent profit. When you become the boss, your business profit is your paycheck. Nothing is permanent in business or in life. I can't remember the last time that a specific idea or strategy worked for longer than six months for any of my businesses. You constantly need to adapt. You can't fully rely on a fad, trend, or mega-trend. Instead, you can rely on a combination of trends and mega-trends, potentially using fads to your advantage along the way.

Once I fully understood the three types of trends, I was then able to see the current bell curves my own business was riding. At that point, I was able to think about what risks there might be with these trends. Hedging comes into play when you select one of these risks and figure out how to protect yourself from that outcome. My biggest concern was that my YouTube channel would somehow disappear into the abyss, or that YouTube would somehow no longer be relevant. For example, even the best radio hosts lost listeners as the mega-trend of personal media devices took over, collapsing the demand for talk radio. While I have had consistent long-term success with YouTube, it was fears like this that led me to hedge against potentially bad outcomes. This meant diversifying revenue streams, creating unrelated businesses, and building a financial fortress within my personal life, among other things.

Hedging is a great strategy, but like any strategy out there, it cannot be relied upon fully. Why is that, you may ask? Human error. When you are sailing your boat, you might not always read the wind or waters correctly. In business, you might not always make the right decisions, even if you correctly identify a fad or a trend. As such, there is an additional strategy that should be layered on top of hedging, and that is diversification. Just like with hedging, I learned about this in my early years too.

Diversification 101

As a kid, I would ask for Legos every Christmas. Some years I asked for multiple smaller Lego sets and other years I wanted one large set. Eventually, I realized that I would always end up feeling disappointed on the years that I asked Santa for the big set because I wouldn't have any other sets left to build during Christmas vacation. I went all in on one big gift, instead of spreading out my good fortune across multiple Lego sets. As the years progressed and my interests broadened to K'Nex, I would practice diversification by asking for many smaller sets, just like with the Legos.

Diversification is the strategy of spreading your eggs across multiple baskets, instead of putting all of them in one. In the investment world, the goal of a well-diversified portfolio is to have your assets moving in different directions at the same time. In an ideal scenario, a loss from one is offset by a gain from another. You have the power to make that happen through diversification in your portfolio as well as in your life and business. Like hedging, you can apply diversification to many areas of life. For example, let's consider my content mix. Most people look at me and think that I only create financial content. While that is mostly true, I have made and continue to make tens of thousands of dollars from content completely unrelated to finance. For example, over the last few years I have made thousands of dollars as an affiliate for various e-book platforms. I have also generated significant revenues from SAAS products, VPNs, web hosting plans, books, and more. Within my investment portfolio, I own different assets like stocks, crypto, NFTs, private equity, precious metals, land, and single-family and multifamily real estate.

For a long time, I was almost exclusively covering investing and finance-related topics on my channel. However, my concerns led me to hedge against a loss of interest in this content by diversifying across different topics. I now view content as a long-term asset, and that influences the type of content I create. I primarily create evergreen content, or content that is searched for consistently over time. My channel has a range of videos, such as "best high-paying jobs," "how to lease a car," "best $0 businesses to start" and more. When creating a video, I usually think about how it will perform over the next one to five years and use Google Trends to validate if it's evergreen. Although some topics may not get a ton of traffic, overall traffic over a few years will bring in thousands of dollars in ad revenue. For example, I have a video on "how to file your taxes" that generates tens of thousands of views and thousands of dollars in commissions every year around tax time. Since I put a lot of time and effort into the video, it is extremely valuable. This has made it relevant year-after-year with a new audience. In addition, the video I did reviewing Audible that is years old earns me hundreds of dollars every month. All of this is possible through capitalizing on trends with evergreen content.

Now, how would something like this apply to a real-life side hustle? I recommend deploying content targeted to local searches for your product or service. For example, if you offer dryer vent cleaning, you could put together a simple website and create articles about topics people might be searching for. If you live in Austin, Texas, you could write an article called "Austin Texas dryer vent cleaning." Within that article, you would cover the most common sources of clogs, be it a mouse nest or a rattlesnake den. After that, you could include a form where people could request more information on your cleaning service. Even if content isn't the focus of your business, you should still use evergreen content strategies like this. Remember, add value first! The most likely outcome is that someone who stumbles upon your article from a Google search will decide that they don't want to take on the project themselves. When you educate them on how to do it, they will realize how challenging it is and decide to hire an expert—you!

Survival of the Fittest

Since there is little permanence in the world of online content, you will find that influencers come and go. It's no different than how movie stars and singers often have a rise to fame, a peak, and then a decline. The question becomes, how do you stay relevant? I was one of the very first people creating educational content related to finance on YouTube. However, that is not why I am still relevant today. Over the years, thousands of others have now followed suit and started their own financial channels on YouTube. Many have surpassed me, some have caught up, and others have not fared well. I'll even be the first to tell you that many of these channels have better production quality, better editing, and more of a "wow" factor. As word spread about how lucrative being a financial influencer is, competition surged. That led to the quality bar being pushed higher and higher. As a result, many financial channels that were relevant in the late 2010s have completely fallen out of favor. In almost every scenario where a full-time creator had a negative outcome, a key issue was a lack of diversification or hedging. It usually goes down like this. The creator followed a strategy that worked well early on, garnering them a large following. Then they repeated that strategy over and over. Eventually, the strategy itself stopped working, meaning they aren't getting the same outcome or result as before. The creator eventually experiences burnout from getting a smaller and smaller reward each time for the same amount of effort as before. Eventually, they give up and stop posting. Let's look at an example of this.

During the global pandemic, there was a surge in channels covering different stimulus packages. While many of these channels grew overnight, most of them failed to diversify their content. Instead, they just created video after video about stimulus package updates. This worked great—until it didn't. The topic turned out to be a fad. As soon as government stimulus curbed back, most of these channels were left in the dust. However, some were able to successfully pivot by transitioning to general news topics. You can certainly use fads to establish yourself, or even bolster your existing audience, but you can't stay there forever. A leap must be made to a longer-term trend.

Since you will mostly be utilizing trends and fads to grow or even sustain your business, it's imperative to spot the differences. Here are some pointers on spotting trends vs. fads:

- **Consider where you learned about this new "thing."** Most fads today are going to spread via social media or mainstream news outlets.
- **Research the topic.** If there is existing content on the subject, it may be a trend. If not, there could be a good reason why nobody has made content. (This was the case with my fidget spinner channel.)
- **Validate the trend with data.** These days, there is so much data available to us. We no longer need to make decisions from assumptions. Google Trends is a completely free tool that lets you view search activity for keywords. Simply type in your search, and you can see a visual chart of the popularity of this search term.

Since a trend is something that takes place over a number of years, you would want to see interest in this search term over time. In an ideal world, the interest would be growing as well. This means you are looking at a growing trend. On the flip side, a declining trend loses interest over time. These should generally be avoided, unless you are able to validate that this is a mega-trend. For example, interest in podcasting was dying off in the early 2010s before podcasts became a social phenomenon in the late 2010s. Podcasting is now a mega-trend, which experiences its own up and down cycles in terms of overall interest.

However, you can likely rely on the fact that there will be tons of people tuning in for many decades to come.

Once you are very familiar with the trends that impact your business, you can ride the cycles. For example, one of the biggest trends that impacts my business is the performance of the stock and cryptocurrency markets, or the ups and downs. When the market is going up and people are making money, interest and participation are high. As a result, my content does well across the board. When the market is going down, participation dwindles. Few people who were participating early on are continuing, as they are now losing money. Since people aren't making money, fewer new people decide to learn about the stock market and investing. Views drop. I have navigated my businesses through two bear markets now, or periods of stock price decline, so I have learned how to adapt to these interest cycles. One of these strategies has been focusing on content that will do well during a bear market. This includes videos on topics like "side hustle ideas."

Hedging 101

In order to stay relevant, you need to define your business by the service, not the medium. Let me elaborate on this. People often tie their brand to the medium they use to provide a particular product or service. For example, instead of limiting my brand to "financial YouTuber," I prefer to call myself a "financial content creator." This distinction is important because it allows me to have an open mind about how I provide my content as well as where I provide it. Initially, I was just shooting videos. Years later, I hedged by creating both audio and written content as well. Had I viewed myself solely as a YouTuber, I would have exclusively made video content. That's all fine and dandy if YouTube stays relevant, but what if it doesn't? User-generated content is the mega-trend here, not YouTube.

The number one risk I was concerned about with my business was platform risk. Sure, I had a large following on YouTube, which enabled me to make money through various avenues. The problem was that I had all of my eggs in one basket. A big following on MySpace was very useful in 2007. A decade later, it was far less valuable. Today, it might be considered worthless by many. In addition, I didn't have a direct line of communication with my audience. Based on the YouTube algorithm, the videos I post only get shared with a select handful of my subscribers. As a result, I'm at the mercy of this algorithm.

So how did I hedge against this? As mentioned before, I started a completely separate blog in which I actually owned the platform I was creating. In 2018, I reached out to an old high school friend who had a background in finance. We drew up plans for a review and comparison site called Investing Simple, based off an Instagram page I had purchased prior. Most financial content out there is too complicated for people to understand; our plan was to create a more accessible financial resource. I already had established relationships with many of these online trading platforms, so I was able to leverage those with this blog as well. In addition to hedging with the blog, I also began collecting names and emails from my YouTube audience by providing free resources. This gave me a direct line of communication with them, something I did not have before

This is one of my favorite strategies: leveraging information, skills, talent, connections, and other resources across multiple businesses I own. There's a good reason why I launched blogs in the finance space and not nutrition, for example. In business, this is referred to as synergy. This is two or more organizations that achieve a combined greater output working together than they would have achieved singularly. This was the case with my YouTube channel and blog, working side by side. We began writing reviews and comparison articles related to these different apps and earned affiliate commissions in the process. I was then able to link to many of these articles from my YouTube channel, driving traffic to the site. During the first few months of operation, nearly all the traffic for the site was directed from my channel. I was also able to repurpose content. If I did a video on a Roth IRA, I could then take that information in the video outline and turn it into an article for Investing Simple with relative ease. This blog was by no means an overnight success. In fact, there was a time in 2019 when we almost shuttered operations because we were losing roughly $1,000 per month on it. However, the blog recovered and grew over time. It is now a huge pillar to my overall online business portfolio. Since then, I've created Farmland Riches, a second investing blog focusing on the prospects of farmland ownership and investment.

I follow the same strategies, but now I share collective resources from my multiple blogs on top of my channel. I am able to link back and forth between my different websites and channels.

Hedging Outside of Business

You need to hedge in both your business and personal financial life if you decide to go full-time with your business. If you work a side hustle alongside your job, you don't really need to hedge unless you want to. That is because your hedge is your job. If you lose the income from your side hustle, you have the income from your job to fall back on.

The main risk you need to hedge against is fluctuating income, or worse, loss of income. When I moved into my first apartment, I was paying $1,400 a month in rent. While I could afford this based on my income at the time, I didn't like the idea of shelling money out on rent and seeing nothing in return. I also wasn't thrilled with the idea of spending around $2,500 on monthly expenses. If my income took a nosedive, I would be burning most of my fuel on rent and other monthly costs. At the time, I was learning a lot from one of my mentors, Graham Stephan. He's an authority on real estate, especially a strategy known as "house hacking." This is where you essentially live for free by offsetting your mortgage with income from rental units. I was a little hesitant about real estate after seeing what my dad went through, but I saw how well this had worked for Graham and decided to follow in his footsteps.

I tried applying for a mortgage in 2018, but I needed to have a longer track record of business activity in order to get approved. It wasn't until early 2019 that I was approved for a mortgage. I ended up finding a great property in my hometown. It had a main house and multiple rental units, a house hack dream. I purchased the place and moved into the main house, inheriting the existing tenants.

Now, how exactly was this a hedge against loss of income? I ended up refinancing shortly after buying the property because I was able to complete a remodel that allowed for more rental income. After that, this is what the numbers looked like:

- Mortgage: $2,475
- Gross Rental Income: $2,075

I was living in a beautiful two-bedroom, two-bathroom house and effectively paying $400 per month. Not to mention, part of my mortgage goes toward equity, so that is really money back in my pocket. I spent about two years living there with this setup, and that allowed me to significantly grow my net worth. I wasn't directing any money toward housing costs, so I was investing most of what I was making into the stock market.

Although I no longer reside in this property, it is still one of the single best investments I have made. It was my first foray into real estate investing and has been a great experience overall. Since then, I've made more investments into this asset. Real estate values have skyrocketed over the years, so the value of this asset has grown tremendously while the mortgage has been paid down primarily through the rental income. In addition, this opened up a whole new avenue of tax deductions and write-offs for myself. Now that I fully rent the property, it is a cash-flow positive investment for me. Real estate also opens the door for a myriad of different side hustles as well. For example, I rented out my spare bedroom on Airbnb, creating an additional revenue stream from my rental property. While it ended up being mostly for the content, this is a viable option for those who have extra space and are looking for a side hustle. Make no mistake: hosting on Airbnb is a decent amount of work!

Keep in mind that you should have a plan for what you are going to do with your money. You are reading this book because you want to bring in extra money each month through a side hustle. Based on the foundation we are building together, you have a great chance of having success. But what you do with that money needs to be an important consideration. I have seen many people earn millions following a fad, only to have the income stream vanish. Meanwhile, they spent all the money on vacations, jewelry, or sports cars. While I've wasted some money on stuff like this, I have been smart with most of what I've earned.

There's no way to accurately predict the future. Each business will have unique offerings and risks. You should aim to identify those risks and hedge against them. Beyond that, you should look at what you are offering and determine what would happen if you're thrown a curveball. For example, if you started a cupcake business, would it be able to survive through a lockdown? This was a challenge faced by businesses all over the world in 2020. You could hedge for this by selling contact-free at-home cupcake kits or offering online orders. With whatever side hustle you pursue, keep in mind that the bell curve you are riding is a trend like anything else. You need to be able to adapt. Starting and even growing a business or a side hustle is one thing. Maintaining it for years is a different one.

Key Takeaways

- Hedging is a risk management strategy that safeguards against a potential negative outcome.
- Diversification is the strategy of spreading your eggs across multiple baskets instead of putting all of your eggs in one.
- Learn how to identify trends, as well as discern the difference among fads, trends, and mega-trends.
- The driving force behind your business is going to be a combination of trends and mega-trends. You can take advantage of fads, but you cannot rely on them.
- Instead of basing your plans off assumptions, use tools like Google Trends to look at existing data. This is called quantitative research.
- You should also consider qualitative research—your own observations as you interact with the real world. Simply ask yourself, what's changing?

Selling Your Business

While it may feel too soon, now is the time to think about whether you want to sell part or all of your business at some point in the future. Here's why. You need to complete some very important steps early on when setting up your business, and the consideration of a future sale will motivate you to do this now. It's far easier to do things right from the beginning rather than trying to fix them later. Imagine building a new house on top of an old, crumbling foundation. If you don't replace the foundation from the start, it will be much more work to do so years later. It is easier to build correctly from the ground up than it is to go back and redo everything later.

If you build your business with the prospect of selling it eventually, you're more likely to do things the right way from day one, just like repairing that old foundation as your first project on a home remodel. I have built multiple businesses from a firm footing following this strategy of keeping the future sale of the business in mind early on. I've learned the right way of doing things as well as the wrong way, mostly through trial and error. What I have found is the differences between a well-organized business and one that is a mess are largely based on how it was launched. It's very clear who did and didn't follow the simple, yet important, steps that I mentioned earlier. We'll get to those shortly. When your ultimate goal is to sell some or all of your business for top dollar, you will find yourself building a better structure from the foundation on up. Keeping the prospect of selling your business in mind will help you be far more organized and proactive while you run your business. There are other benefits to selling equity in your business too, beyond just being able to keep track of things better.

Why Sell Equity in Your Business?

Before we get into the steps I recommend taking, let's discuss why someone, potentially you, would sell some or all of their business. Selling an ownership stake in your business has many advantages. One of the biggest is that it allows for potential diversification, which was covered in the previous chapter. You could take on a partner, collect a cash windfall, and invest that money in an unrelated industry as a hedge. Keep in mind that this isn't the new partner investing into your business—this is them purchasing equity in the business from you, the owner. If they were investing in your business, the cash would go into the business. Since the money goes to you, you are free to do whatever you want with it. The possibilities of hedging with proceeds from selling a business are endless. For example, you could build a business up, sell off some of it, and invest in a rental property, providing you with an additional revenue stream. Plan to make the most of this opportunity!

I decided to sell off part of my blog Farmland Riches in 2021 to diversify my investment portfolio as well as bring on some strategic partners to further grow the business. I used some of that money from the sale to buy a piece of land situated on a quiet, peaceful pond in upstate New York. My plan is to use it as a recreational camping lot and a destination for friends and family gatherings. I can also use this land at any point to make money, allowing for this to be a hedge as well. Apps like Hipcamp let you rent out campsites on your land, just like Airbnb. It's mind-blowing to think that a digital site I created in late 2020 ended up buying me a piece of land, free and clear, that I can keep in my family forever. As I own the land, or make improvements to it, it will continue to go up in value. Also, through good planning, I still own the biggest stake in the blog, so the revenue is still coming in.

Why Give Away Equity in Your Business?

Here's another strategy to consider. It is common in the world of business to bring on a new partner in an existing business without having that individual purchase equity from you. Instead, you give it to them. In this case, the new partner is going to provide some type of benefit to the entire operation. For example, when we took on our third partner, Andrew "Apple" Crider, with Investing Simple, he was going to launch a YouTube channel for us. While we gave him a percentage of our existing revenue, he created a brand-new revenue stream for us that generates thousands monthly. The benefit of bringing him on made more money for the existing partners in the business.

Overall, Investing Simple benefited tremendously through the addition of our third partner. We created a brand-new revenue stream for the business.

Farmland Riches has become a more successful operation through joint promotional efforts of the owners as well as back-end improvements. For example, one of the new partners knows coding, so we were able to add a Farmland Return Calculator to our site that is quite popular. This, in turn, brings people to the site and makes us more money. Without a partner with this know-how, I would've had to do it myself or hire someone to do it, costing thousands.

Cons of Business Partnerships

There are some cons associated with selling off part of your business or bringing on more partners down the line. One negative is that you are surrendering your ability to have full control. It may be frustrating to have your business partners veto an idea of yours when you would have run with it on your own. You don't want to have too many people involved with decision-making. I recommend bringing on one to four partners for a business venture, but no more. Otherwise, you will undoubtedly have too many cooks in the kitchen.

You also have the potential for the nightmare situation of having a deadbeat business partner. Thankfully, this has never happened to me. However, it has happened to some close friends of mine. In this scenario, you usually have two or more people in a business all with equal ownership and duties. The business starts bringing in revenue and all is well. A year later, one of your business partners ghosts. They stop responding to emails, texts, and direct messages. At the end of the quarter, they send a short text that reads, "I want my check." This usually leads to a lot of arguing and even potential litigation. During this time, the business inevitably suffers. Sometimes it ends up worthless in the end as the entire operation falls apart during the feud. Bringing someone into business with you is not a decision that should be taken lightly.

Get Out of the Driver's Seat!

There was a time when I built houses on lousy foundations. What I mean by that is I didn't always build things correctly from the ground up in business. A lot of what I am going to share with you is based on my personal experiences—also known as mistakes. One of those was a pivotal moment when I was politely called out by a podcast host. When I was interviewed on Cody Loughlin's *Money Talkers* show, Cody asked me what a typical day in my life looks like. I told him it really varied. Sometimes I was spending an entire day editing content from our team of writers, adding in links, creating blog featured images, and scheduling articles. Other days, I might not do anything work-related at all. Instead, I might be out practicing my swing at the driving range. He then asked me if I enjoyed those aspects of my business, and I told him those things fall into the category of necessary evils for me and my business partner. Essentially, I did these things because I needed to do them, or else the business would not function. My business partner did another handful of tasks like this, such as logging our financials in spreadsheets.

After the show was done, off the record, Cody asked me why the heck I was doing tasks like editing and scheduling articles if I didn't enjoy it. Or why my partner was logging data in spreadsheets. The question really caught me off guard, and I didn't have any good answer. Prior to this, my answer was because I had to do them. I was now having my belief system challenged, realizing that perhaps I didn't need to be doing these things. Cody then asked me what my long-term plan was with the Investing Simple blog. I told him that years down the line, my plan was to sell it for millions of dollars. He then asked me one of the most important questions I have ever been asked: "Would you go work for whoever ended up purchasing the blog?" My answer was, of course, a resounding no. At that point, the message Cody was trying to bring home clicked.

My business partner and I had successfully built Investing Simple as an owner-operated business. This type of business is extremely difficult to sell, as the buyer has to either find an operator or become the operator of the business. Not to mention, if we plan on selling our blog for millions of dollars, that buyer is more than likely looking to buy it as an investment that produces cash flow. Think about it this way: Would you rather buy a coffee shop that has a manager or one where the new owner (you) has to manage it? Most, if not all, would prefer the managed shop. Cody explained that owner-operated businesses usually come with a much lower price tag due to these factors. He encouraged me to get out from behind the driver's seat of operations and instead focus on hiring people and creating systems. I approached my business partners, and they were all on board with the idea.

We spent weeks putting pen to paper, drafting digital versions of standard operating procedures (SOPs), documenting processes and creating workflows for every department. Instead of having one person taking care of all of these different functions, we divided the roles across various departments like writing, editing, and affiliate link management. This was a tremendous undertaking at first, but it led to the blog becoming more of a self-operating business. After we created the systems, we simply had to bring on the right team. This meant hiring talented freelancers looking to work hourly or get paid by word count for writing. This took some time, and there were a few who were not the best fit. However, it ultimately led to a more independent and passive business, rather than an active operation in which we were highly involved. It's not entirely hands-off at this point in time, but the business is also not fully reliant on any of the owners to function. This has enabled us to make more money, as we can now spend time growing the business, not just running it. I now have multiple businesses with multiple partners. My personal brand, however, is still fully owned by me. Overall, it has been a great decision to bring on additional partners. Even if you don't plan on doing this now, you at least understand the importance of building things right from the ground up. These are the things every successful business needs.

1. EMAIL ACCOUNTS

Your business should have a unique email address associated with it. No, not a Gmail address. It needs to be your name or the department followed by your business website URL. For example, I could use ryan@mywebsite. com. Although your content can show some personality, your email address should not. Think back to Lesson 2: Dress Yourself (and Your Business) for Success.

Beyond that, you should have a completely separate email account for every one of your businesses. How would you sell a business, or even keep things organized, if all of the logins go back to your personal email? If you have a specific email just for your business, you can simply hand over the password to the new owner. Having different mailboxes by department also shows a potential buyer that your business is professional and well organized. For example, you could have a help@yourwebsite.com email for customer service inquiries.

2. WEB HOSTING

Every business out there needs a website. A self-hosted website is your best option, as it is often the most cost-effective in the long run. This involves hosting your website content on the internet. A web host is simply a platform for which you pay a monthly fee in order to broadcast your website and related files to the internet. You're essentially renting space, rather than buying your own server.

If you decide to pursue blogging, it's very possible you will have multiple sites someday. I encourage you to have a separate web hosting account for each site. During the sale, you will be able to hand over the credentials to your web host platform instead of going through the process of transferring the site to their plan. All of this makes for a much more efficient and seamless transaction.

3. SOCIAL MEDIA

You will need to create a separate login for each social media profile. If both your personal and business Instagram are tethered to your personal email or phone number, how would you be able to hand your business page over to someone else? As someone who has bought and sold Instagram pages in the past, I can tell you that this is a huge consideration. Right now, you're probably focused on building a business, but even if you don't think you have any plans on selling, it is a simple step that could save you from a massive headache in the future. You can't always rely on customer service either; who's to say that you could even get hold of Instagram to transfer an account to someone else? You could create a massively successful Instagram page but have no way of selling it if it's tied to your personal email or phone number.

Another huge consideration is guarding against cyber threats, like password breaches. I recommend storing all passwords within a secure vault. This keeps all your logins in one place, and you are authenticated each time you need to automatically retrieve a login. A password vault will notify you if you have reused a password too many times or if it's been involved in a breach. This should go without saying, but if you launch multiple businesses over time, each one should have its own password vault account that can be handed over during a sale.

4. OPERATING PROCEDURES

Let's talk more about procedures now. While it may not be the most exciting part of launching a successful business, I highly recommend documenting procedures for your business operations as you go. One of the most common pitfalls business owners run into is simply doing things themselves because they are "too busy" to show someone else how to do it. If you have to walk someone through the process of doing something while you do it, it's going to take much longer. Also, you will likely need to watch over them or check their work while they get the entire process down. What a huge waste of time, right? No! Spending time coaching or training your team is always a valuable investment. It's a way to get an immediate return on investment, but you need to be patient. Having standard operating procedures (SOPs) in place will allow you to step back from a lot of the training process rather than verbally explaining something.

Most business owners or side hustlers out there do not have any formal standard operating procedures written out. As a result, the act of hiring people or even bringing on an independent contractor becomes a frustrating experience. Typically, people bring on more help when needed, not beforehand. The problem with hiring because you are too busy is that you now need to spend your limited time training new employees. But what if you had simply documented processes and steps back before you were busy? You could simply hand over these procedures to your new staff and answer any questions they have as they go. In my businesses, we have taken this a step further by creating video training for our writers.

I recommend starting out with a cloud-based document that can be shared as well as changed over time. I prefer Google Docs for this. SOPs can be as simple as numbered steps with bullet points further explaining them. As you complete different tasks related to your business, create these easy-to-follow documents for others to reference in the future.

5. FACE VS. NO FACE

Next, you should consider whether you plan on being the face of your business. I learned another very important lesson about this from Jeff Rose, one of my blogging mentors. (Fun fact: he's the reason I started Investing Simple in the first place!) Jeff has a YouTube channel of his own as well as very popular personal finance blog, Good Financial Cents. In addition to this site, Jeff has some other blogs, including a site where he sells life insurance leads called LifeInsuranceByJeff.com. I remember him telling me how he regrets being the name of this site. Nobody other than Jeff Rose or another Jeff could feasibly operate the site. Now of course, you could get around this with ghostwriters and other things like that. However, the site being all about "Jeff" certainly devalues it somewhat, as it makes it difficult for someone else to come in and take the wheel.

One of the most important technical factors in the blogging world is domain authority. You might think that you could simply change the domain name of a site during the sale, but that would in turn mean losing the associated domain authority. All the brand equity or social value the brand has would be lost in the process. You may want to be the face of your business now, but will that be the case in five or 10 years? Would you eventually want to have other people creating content for your online platforms? These are all careful considerations that should be made at the inception of your business.

6. RETAIN CONTROL

It's important to think about this at the onset to consider what percentage of the business you want to retain yourself. I've never fully divested one of my businesses to someone else, but there is a possibility of this in the future for one of my blogs. In general, I like the constant challenges of being involved with my different ventures, so selling something off completely doesn't really appeal to me.

Here's an example of this in action. I sold off most of the equity in the Farmland Riches blog in 2021, yet I retained 50 percent voting rights. There are two partners who invested with voting rights and two partners with nonvoting rights who have a smaller chunk. I wanted to remain in a position in which I could say no to an idea if I didn't like it. Had I only retained a minority voting position, I would have effectively lost voting control of the business. With this setup, I need approval from at least one of the two voting partners in order to proceed. Similarly, they each need my approval for an idea, even one they collectively agree on. I've seen situations where individuals sell off a majority stake in their business while still being involved in the operations. This can become problematic if you disagree with the direction of the business, as you no longer have control. Your partners could effectively run your creation into the ground with that type of business structure.

7. OPERATING AGREEMENT

You should always create an operating agreement that is reviewed or, better yet, written by an attorney. An operating agreement is a legal document that outlines important information, such as who the owners are, what percentages they own, and so forth. It also clearly lays out the terms of the arrangement. Too many times now I have seen friends get in trouble because of loose business agreements—or because they have no agreement in place whatsoever.

Regardless of whether you plan to sell your business, you should have a contract associated with almost all work you are doing for others. People tend to go into business with their friends or even family members. What they often forget is that a business is a long-term commitment. For example, as mentioned earlier, what if one of the partners decides to stop doing any work but still wants to get paid? This is something that could be addressed in an operating agreement with some type of plan or clause if a partner stops contributing as agreed upon. Although contracts and agreements may seem like an unnecessary waste of time, they are crucial to have in place when you need to fall back on them. Like insurance, it is important to have agreements in place in the rare event you need to use them. "Hope for the best, prepare for the worst," as my dad taught me.

8. BUSINESS STRUCTURE

If you are investing in a business yourself or selling part or all of it, you need to have a formal business entity in place. This is referred to as an LLC, which stands for Limited Liability Company. You should never give someone money toward a business idea if there isn't an operating agreement, a subsequent LLC, and a bank account in place. In turn, you should not expect to sell part or all of a business without these in place either.

Luckily, you can form an LLC for less than $500 in most states. When I sold off equity in Farmland Riches, I had an operating agreement drafted for $1,500. For a total of $2,000, I had a legitimate business that could be invested into. Each partner is listed as a member on the LLC. If you plan on taking on an equity partner in the future, you can adjust the ownership percentages and members associated with an LLC. We did this when we took on our third strategic partner at Investing Simple in 2020.

9. BANK ACCOUNT

Once you have a separate legal entity for your business, which is an LLC in most cases, the next step is to open a business bank account. It's okay to launch a side hustle out of your personal bank account, but once you start making a few thousand dollars a month, it's time to separate this income and open a business bank account.

All you need to open a business bank account is an LLC paired with an Employer Identification number (EIN). The only cost associated with this is the establishment of the LLC. The EIN, which is basically like a Social Security number for a business, is provided free by the

United States government for tax purposes. Keep in mind that a business being operated out of a personal bank account is not one that can be invested into. It's also dangerous from a legality perspective, as you have no separation between yourself and your business. If you were to be sued for some reason, that person could easily go after your personal assets. Having a business bank account with separate personal and business transactions adds a layer of protection here, separating your personal assets from the business assets. In this case, the person suing you would likely only be able to go after your business assets.

Instead of building a business on a lousy foundation, you now have the tools necessary to build things correctly from the ground up. Keeping the prospect of selling your business in mind will help you to accomplish this. It's kind of like owning a sports car. I'll admit, I've owned a couple. The first was a 2009 Nissan GT-R, and the second was a 2018 Mercedes Benz AMG E63S. While I did lose a little money on these cars, it wasn't much compared to the high value of the vehicles and the overall experience of owning them. This was because I kept the idea of selling them in mind from day one. This accomplished two things. First, it led me to do my research and purchase cars that retain value well. Second, I kept both in immaculate condition. From day one, have an exit strategy for assets. A business or a car is no exception.

Doing all of this can be an exhaustive process, especially documenting business procedures. And because you'll adapt to changing trends, these procedures will need to be updated over time. However, it's worth the investment of time and effort up front to have an efficient, well-established business. Once the work is done, you will have your business all packed up like a well-organized suitcase, ready to go anywhere. If you decide you want to sell some or all of it, you are ready to roll right now.

Key Takeaways

- Don't build a business with a shaky foundation! Start out solid so it can be worth more in the future.

- Selling part of your business opens the door for potential diversification. You could take on a partner, collect a cash windfall, and invest that money in a different industry as a hedge.

- When you bring in investors, you may no longer be in the driver's seat, and this can be unsettling for some people. But use that newfound time to pursue other money-making opportunities.

- It's vital to write down standard operating procedures (SOPs) that document processes and create workflows for every department.

- Any business arrangement should have a well-defined operating agreement. Ideally, this should be prepared by an attorney.

- Establish your business as a legal entity by creating a Limited Liability Company (LLC). This will cost under $500 if it's a single-member business.

- With an LLC, all you need is an Employer Identification Number (EIN) to open a business bank account, giving you important organization of finances and potential legal protection too.

The Time to Start Is Now

There's a famous quote from Warren Buffet: "Someone's sitting in the shade today because someone planted a tree a long time ago." I used to believe this quote was about retirement, about how planting a tree (making an investment) and watering it (contributing money over time) would allow you to relax decades from now. Once I started my own side hustle, this quote took on a new meaning for me. At the utility company, I was following the traditional retirement understanding of this quote, stashing away a bit each week into my 401(k). I could've retired by age 50 as a multimillionaire. But I knew that life wasn't for me.

Today, I look at each piece of content I post as a seed that I am planting. Some will grow into strong, tall plants providing amazing shade. Others may not even sprout. The trees that provide shade are the pieces of evergreen content that I own or create, providing consistent monthly income. Planting a tree does not only mean investing money, a resource that many are lacking. It can also mean investing time, energy, and resources into a side hustle. I was able to take a calculated risk and leave my job, jumping off and sailing into the unknown. Keep in mind that this came after a six-month transition period during which I carefully planned everything, especially the financial aspect of giving up my primary income source at the time. This move paid off well in the long run and allowed me to become a millionaire in my twenties by catching a trend early and learning how to ride the waves.

All of this is possible for you as well, but only if you *start*. The simple decision to pick up a camera and shoot very basic videos from my car kicked off my new life. That is where I started—in a Walmart parking lot, shooting videos on a cheap camera in my beat-up SUV. It's up to you where your new life journey begins. All it takes is the first step—getting started with that launch fuel. Then allow long-term consistency to take over. Pick an idea and get going on an MVP.

When I took that leap by quitting my job, I had help and reassurance from my mentor, Jake. I could call him up and ask for a pep talk anytime. So here's my pep talk for you. No, don't quit your job. Instead, hit the pavement, grab the camera, or open the laptop. Not tomorrow, not next week. Right now, today. Today, the doors are open wider than ever before to people who are just starting out. Plant your seed by investing in yourself. Finding the confidence to take that first step to start a business is one of the best investments you will ever make. In fact, you have already made a massive investment in yourself by making it to the end of this book. You are armed with a powerful set of tools, tactics, and a brand-new outlook on what is possible in this world. The only thing you have to do now is get going and keep moving.

How to Remain Consistent

As you now know, the two most important resources you have control over are your time and your money. Often, a lack of capital holds people back from putting boots to the ground. But a side hustle can be an investment that requires very little of your money. So even if you don't have a lot of money right now, that isn't a problem. You have the time, or the ability to make time. Following the strategies covered in Lesson 5, you can free up at least an hour a day. Even if you take Sundays off, you can accomplish a lot with a consistent six hours a week. As far as the money side of things goes, get creative. I could have held myself back from starting my channel until I invested thousands into production equipment. Instead, I bootstrapped; I used what I had in front of me right then and there. I filmed in my car with a cheap digital camera that I already owned. By bootstrapping, you can get up and get started with your side hustle regardless of your limited resources. That covers the launch fuel side of things, but how do you then remain consistent after the new factor wears off?

A side hustle requires a consistent investment of your time, not just a one-time investment. Like with the stock market, it is the consistent contribution that brings you long-term success. However, that consistency doesn't necessarily mean investing a lot of time each day. Think about the amount of time you spend gaming, texting, or watching Netflix. Why not use that time for a better purpose? For example, if you start a blog and consistently write one article per week, you would have over 500 articles in 10 years. I have about 1,000 pieces of different content on the internet that I fully or partially own through different business ventures. This took me six years to build. I am in my position because I don't allow myself to become complacent, and neither can you. Use your time to test new things and to find and utilize changing trends to your advantage. You can't just plant a seed, water it, and walk away. You have to consistently water it and frequently weed out anything that keeps it from flourishing.

Let's say you decide to start a landscaping side hustle. Unless you form a partnership right out of the gate, your landscaping business will likely be a one-person operation. You alone will be making the calls, clipping the grass, and putting gas in the equipment. But over time, as your client base grows and profits increase, you will be able to hire more employees. At that point, you can focus on revving up the business and overseeing the work. People tend to keep the same landscaper for many years. If your prices and quality are consistent, you can build up a portfolio of regular clients. If you cut grass year-round and grow your client base by one new client every two weeks, you will have 26 clients. In five years, this will grow to 130 people paying you every single month. As your portfolio of clients grows, so do your profits and, eventually, your business.

If you're just starting your side hustle, you don't need to know how to do everything yet. All you need is enough information to complete step one, starting your side hustle. After that, you can evaluate and learn. You can accomplish so much by being consistent and putting in the time and effort. A lot of aspiring entrepreneurs make the mistake of mapping out every single step they have to complete at the onset of a new project. This could easily lead to a list that is pages long. I don't know about you, but I would find that extremely demotivating. This type of planning falls under the category of analysis paralysis. You can't afford to waste time like this. Take action one step at a time.

You Can Do This

You may see successful people and think that they've done something spectacular or truly one of a kind. Maybe you even think that about me or other social media influencers. I can't speak for everyone, but I can tell you that I didn't do anything spectacular or even that unique to reach where I am today. I simply identified an opportunity and ran with it. I'm not even the only one from my hometown who did this. Some close friends of mine have done the same, following directly in my footsteps.

After seeing the success I had over the years, my video editor Jake Carlini decided to follow many of the same strategies covered in this book. In 2020, he launched his own YouTube channel. He decided to go into the entertainment space, one of the most competitive content niches out there. YouTube was oversaturated in 2020, especially in the entertainment category. Even so, Jake was able to make it by consistently working and adapting over the years. He would have encountered even more competition had he started later. I'm not saying this to demotivate you; I'm saying this to convey why you need to start *now*. Jake Carlini is where he is today because he planted that seed back in 2020. The market is only going to get more competitive with time, not less.

I also know many people who have had tremendous success with side hustles outside of the online world. For example, my friend Nick Furnia started selling homemade cold-brew coffee at school. After graduating high school, he decided to open up his own coffee and crepe shop called Nomad Coffee & Crepes. He has since launched Knockabout Coffee Roasters, under which he ships orders across the country, and has moved into a larger space for his retail coffee shop. Although Nick has accomplished much, most of his success came from starting early and remaining consistent.

What my friends and I did started with very simple actions. Nick brewed coffee at home and sold it out of his backpack at school. I shot videos in a car behind a Walmart on my lunch break. Jake borrowed my camera equipment when I wasn't using it. Once you close this book, time is going to move on like it always has. In fact, it might even move a little bit faster each year that goes by. So, why wouldn't you want to make the most of this time you have and start your own simple action?

My Life Today

I planted a seed years ago, in the form of my YouTube channel. But I didn't just stick to one tree. Over the years, I began diversifying and hedging to prepare for all types of outcomes. This meant planting numerous trees, all overlapping to provide consistent shade. Then, diversifying into entirely different businesses each with many unrelated income streams. Of course, there will be times when lightning strikes a tree branch. But as long as you keep watering your tree, new branches will grow back to replace the old one that came crashing down.

This book is just the beginning of your journey. Treat it like your companion on this adventure, and don't forget to refer back to it. You now have all the tools and information you need to succeed. All that I ask of you in return is to light someone else's torch when the time comes. In the same way that I helped my friends with their ventures, you should do the same with others who decide to follow in your footsteps. Help others plant their seeds, and years later, they'll be relaxing in the shade right next to you.

In the end, all your success will start with one simple action. Take the first step, and then keep moving.

Ready to start your side hustle?
Connect with Ryan and join a community of readers at
sidehustleconnect.com

Acknowledgments

The author would like to thank the following individuals and team members for their support.

Cari Scribner

Stephan Scribner

Taylor Provost

Sasha Scribner

Nick Scribner

Kathy Ordway

Pete Ordway

Sheldon Scribner

John Romano

Ben Scribner

Jake Woodard

Andrew "Apple" Crider

Ed Canty

Nate O'Brien

Jeff Rose

Deacon Hayes

Jordan Kilburn

Cody Loughlin

Marko Zlatic

Brian Jung

The M1 Finance Team

Sebastian Fung

Jaspreet Singh

Charlie Chang

Derik Rutigliano

Spencer Tacy

Vitaliy Volpov

Jeremy Lefebvre

Jack Chapple

Ann Barton

Tamanna Bhasin

Raffi Arslanian

Index

Woodard, Jake, 141–148

milestones, setting, 160–162
MLM (multi-level
  marketing) businesses,
  186–188
money as fuel source,
  101–104. *See also* finances
Money Talkers podcast,
  241–242
motivation, interests and, 35
MVP (Minimum Viable
  Product), 160
    dating app example,
      162–164
    emotions about ideas,
      169–170
    real world example,
      166–169
    testing ideas, 164–166

N

niche areas, content and,
  38–40
niche blogging, 127–129
"No" as response, delayed
  gratification and, 60–63
Nomad Coffee & Crepes,
  260
Norton LifeLock, 246

O

O'Brien, Nate, 39

one-legged stool revenue
  stream problem, 201–202
online audience growth,
  179–180
operating agreement, 250
operating procedures,
  246–247
overhead, 210
owner-operator businesses,
  242–244

P

partnerships, 211, 239–240
pay yourself first, 108–110
paycheck-to-paycheck
  living, 99–100
perception, 43–44
    business appearance,
      54–56
    dress style, 44–46
    personal appearance,
      46–50
    representation, truth in,
      81–82
    routines and, 52–53
    skills and, 50–52

personal appearance, 44–50
personal mentorship, 140
pets, business start-up and,
  67–68
phone, distraction
  elimination, 71–73
phone calls
    follow-up email,
      111–112